COMEDY WRITING

COMEDY WRITING

For Television and Hollywood

Milt Josefsberg

HARPER & ROW, PUBLISHERS, New York
Cambridge, Philadelphia, San Francisco, Washington
London, Mexico City, São Paulo, Singapore, Sydney

FIRST EDITION

Designer: C. Linda Dingler
Copyeditor: Ann Finlayson

Library of Congress Cataloging-in-Publication Data

Josefsberg, Milt, 1911–
Comedy writing for television and Hollywood.

  1. Comedy programs—Authorship.   2. Television
authorship.   3. Moving-picture authorship.   4. Comedy
films—Authorship.   I. Title
PN1992.8.C66J67   1987   808'.066791   86-46073
ISBN 0-06-055070-8   87 88 89 90 91 MPC 10 9 8 7 6 5 4 3 2 1
ISBN 0-06-096086-8 (pbk.)   87 88 89 90 91 MPC 10 9 8 7 6 5 4 3 2 1

To all the writers I've ever worked with—
To all the comedians, comediennes and shows
I've ever worked for—
And, of course,
To Hilda

Contents

Foreword

by Norman Lear

Reader, beware: This will be an unabashed mash note.

I have known, or known of, Milt Josefsberg my entire career. When I started as a writer in the industry, Milt was envied for his long-term involvements with such major comics as Bob Hope and Jack Benny. He followed these prestigious positions with equally impressive credits on Lucille Ball's *Lucy* and *Here's Lucy* series, spent five years on *All in the Family,* and worked as producer and/or executive script consultant on Garry Marshall's three series, *La Verne and Shirley, Mork and Mindy,* and *Happy Days.* That list reads like a history of top-rated sitcoms, as each of those shows was frequently number one in the National Neilsens during Josefsberg's tenure.

I really got to know Milt in the spring of 1975 when we needed an additional story editor on *AITF,* which by then had been on the air for four years. The series was enjoying high ratings as well as high morale, and we needed another talented writer who would fit in with cast and crew, as well as cope with emergencies. Discreet inquiries about Milt made to performers, producers and writers who had worked with and for him, brought one common response: working with Milt was not only a pleasant experience, but an educational one.

My faith in Milt was well rewarded. He came on in 1975,

wrote eleven scripts in his first season, and worked on rewrites of every script we shot that year. After that first season,
Milt became Producer, Head Writer, and Script Consultant,
turning down the Executive Producer post so that he could
devote all his energies to his first love—writing. Over the next
four years, Milt's contributions to scripts and story conferences were immeasurable. He also proved to be invaluable
when it came to collaborating with the new potential staff
writers, several of whom went on to become term writers of
the show, largely thanks to Milt's patience and direction.

On September 17, 1978, I had the honor of presenting to
Milt (and Mort Lachman) an Emmy Award for producing the
Best Comedy Series of that year—*All in the Family.* By that
time, more of Milt's time was spent rewriting than writing
scripts, so when the nominations for Outstanding Writing in
a Comedy Series were announced and three of the four, including the winner, were from *AITF,* Milt shared in the glory
again.

I cannot imagine anyone more qualified to write a book on
comedy writing than Milt Josefsberg. He has taught at colleges, won practically every major award in broadcasting,
received numerous Emmy nominations and Writer's Guild
Awards, and has written every type of comedy known to man
—from Bob Hope's one-liner monologues and sketches to
side-splitting *Lucy* slapstick to some of the most serious and
controversial *All in the Family* episodes ever aired.

You may not know that Milt is also the author of the best-
selling, critically-acclaimed definitive biography of Jack
Benny, *The Jack Benny Show: The Life and Times of America's
Best-Loved Entertainer,* which went into four printings. In
Bob Hope's foreword to the book he writes, "Josefsberg, with
his capacity for total recall, brings us this witty, perceptive
portrait . . ." Hope was not only right about the book—I enjoyed it immensely—he was more than right about Milt's total
recall. Milt leaves none of the most helpful and pertinent facts

about comedy writing out of this book. Those insights, together with the benefit of Milt's vast experience, with a lot of old gags and new humor thrown in, make *Comedy Writing: For Television and Hollywood* a must read for aspiring comedy writers and fans everywhere.

Preface

by Garry K. Marshall

Frequently, in interviews, I mention Milt Josefsberg as one of my mentors, so it is indeed a pleasure to introduce him to you. I learned many valuable lessons in comedy writing from him and I'm sure this book will help teach some of them to you.

I first met Milt in the summer of 1962 when he joined the Joey Bishop situation comedy as head writer and script consultant. I was on staff as a junior writer for the show. Although I was comparatively new in the business, I had heard of Milt because he was already a legend in the industry with his track record of serving nineteen years with two of the giants, Jack Benny and Bob Hope. It was the ambition of every budding writer to be on the staff of either of these two great comedians. In fact, in Neil Simon's latest hit, "Broadway Bound," laid in the late 1940s, he has his semi-biographical counterpart, an aspiring writer, say he'd like to be like Milt Josefsberg and the other Benny writers.

In my first days of association with Milt I was slightly in awe of him; careful of anything I suggested for the scripts lest I say something stupid. Milt considered my contributions quite carefully. Before discarding anything, he analyzed it and tried to find something worthwhile in it, which he frequently did. Some of my ideas and plot twists he used exactly as I wrote them. On others he gave me revisions and new approaches, and when I rewrote them, the improved versions frequently found their way into the script.

At the end of the first season Milt was promoted to Producer and was slated to receive two solo credit cards, one reading "Produced by Milt Josefsberg," and the other, "Script Consultant: Milt Josefsberg." Before our second season started, Milt called me into his office to show me the credit cards. They read, "Produced by Milt Josefsberg" and "Script Consultants: Milt Josefsberg and Garry K. Marshall." Milt not only shared his knowledge with me, he shared that which people guard most zealously, his credit. It was his own idea done over the objection of some executives with the series. This points out another lesson I learned from Milt, and always followed: share credit with those who deserve it.

Milt next joined Lucille Ball's *Lucy* show where he became head writer and the only writer on the staff. It was Milt's job to not only write several shows himself, but to hire freelance writers, set stories with them, and then polish their scripts.

At that time, I had just teamed up with my longtime collaborator, Jerry Belson, and we signed a multiple assignment deal with Milt to write six scripts for *Lucy.* When we'd drop off our first drafts, Milt would go over them several times, making copious notes with each of his readings. He'd mark off entire sections which he liked, but when he came to something he wasn't sure of, he gave us several ideas of how it might possibly be improved. After his secretary had typed his notes, which ran quite a few pages, Jerry and I would meet with him and discuss all revisions pro and con, then we'd do the final draft. One week, we came in and found that Milt's notes ran well over twenty pages. After he handed them to us, Jerry hefted them in his hand and said, "Milt, I've got a great idea—let's throw out the script and shoot the notes." Then we told Milt how much we appreciated his time and suggestions, and that the head writers or producers of most other shows we wrote for gave us suggestions for improving our scripts with such all-embracing instructions as: "Make this sharper," "Make this more pertinent," "Make this better," "Make this funnier." But they never gave us concrete suggestions. Milt and one or two others, like Carl Reiner, gave us specific notes, which helped us tremendously.

When Jerry Belson and I were producing *The Odd Couple*, we tried to hire Milt to head up our writing staff, but Lucille Ball had him tied to a contract. He stayed with her for eight years.

A few years later, when I had *Happy Days, LaVerne and Shirley*, and *Mork and Mindy*, I once again tried to hire Milt, but now he was head writer, producer, and script consultant on *All in the Family*. Fortunately, this was a short-term job for Milt. He was able to leave after only five years.

Milt joined my shows at Paramount in 1980, and although I wanted him to serve on all three of them, he didn't want to spread himself too thin and concentrated on *LaVerne and Shirley*, and *Mork and Mindy* as either Producer or Executive Script Consultant. (When *Mork and Mindy* went off the air, Milt moved back to *Happy Days*.)

He worked on every phase of script development from inception to taping, but what seemed to please him most was working with the several junior writers I had on each series in addition to the three or four experienced scripters. Milt's office and ear were always open to all. He made a point of taking every one of the budding writers, singly or in groups, to lunch several times a season. He would listen to their problems, help them straighten out a story line, punch up a routine, and answer their frequent questions.

At the end of each season, almost every writer, veteran or neophyte, sent Milt notes thanking him for his valuable assistance and contributions. And I was frequently told by the writers how much they felt they learned from working with and listening to Milt.

I know numerous highly respected writers in the industry

who either got their initial start or polished their skills under Milt's guidance. If there is any practitioner of the art who is qualified to teach comedy writing via a book, that person is Milt Josefsberg.

Acknowledgments

The author wishes to thank the following people for their assistance in obtaining permission to use certain verbatim excerpts from television and motion picture scripts: Howard Barton, Virginia Carter, Fred de Cordova, Elliott Kozak, Fran McConnell, Michael A. Miller, Gary Morton, Edwin Perlstein, David Tebet, and Leo Ziffrin.

Also thanks to my two secretaries, Beverly Gray and Ann Clark, who deciphered and retyped my sloppy copy with amazing accuracy.

And finally to those who helped me with research, technical and legal advice: Sheldon Bardach, Mort Fleischmann, Alan Roy Josefsberg, Steven Kent Josefsberg and Al Rylander.

Special and most grateful thanks to:

Maurice Zolotow who, from our days together on the editorial staff of Brooklyn's New Utrecht High School magazine *The Comet*, has laughed at practically everything I said or wrote, and who encouraged me to write comedy.

Russell Galen of the Scott Meredith Literary Agency, who found an outline of my idea for a book on comedy writing in 1978, and for nearly ten years has been encouraging me, in fact "noodging" me, to write this book—and always giving me sage advice.

And finally, a comparatively new friend and associate who

influenced me enormously, Daniel Bial, my editor at Harper & Row. Dan was always there when I needed him. He helped me constantly with valuable suggestions. But most of all I'm thankful to him for doing the most meaningful cutting job on me since I was eight days old.

Author's Introduction

There are several reasons why a person would want to write a comedy for television. One big reason is money. A moderately successful scriptwriter is assured of all the ulcers of the upper brackets. If he or she sells six to eight comedy scripts per year to the various series that are on the air, the reward is roughly from $60,000 to $75,000. And that is just "front" money. Eventually there are "residuals."

Remember residuals. Forget Funk & Wagnalls' definition. To a writer, residual means money. If a series is successful and rerun many times, the residuals on each episode can bring another several thousand dollars per episode to the writers.

Although residuals are wonderful, they are peanuts compared to the rewards raked in by the favored few who own a piece or percentage of the show. And most of the comedy series are owned in part, or in total, by writers.

High on the long list of writers turned moguls are Norman Lear, Garry Marshall, Susan Harris, Ed Weinberger and Gary David Goldberg, all with several successful series. Danny Arnold sired many shows, but his big one was *Barney Miller.* Rumor had it that the amount he received when he sold the show for syndication ran well into eight figures. Gary Nardino, once head honcho at Paramount Pictures, told me that the eventual returns on *LaVerne and Shirley* would outgross the combined totals of *The Godfather* and *Godfather Two*. That was several years ago. Currently, the eventual income on hits like *The Bill Cosby Show, Family Ties, Golden Girls,* and others will be even greater.

Many writers have found their fortunes in variety series and specials. The variety show used to be the backbone of broadcasting. Milton Berle started it all. Milton was followed by such stars as Sid Caesar, Jackie Gleason, Jack Benny, Garry Moore, Dinah Shore, Carol Burnett, Tennessee Ernie Ford, Andy Williams, Flip Wilson, Danny Thomas, Dean Martin and Jerry Lewis, and Dan Rowan and Dick Martin. The list seems endless. Today the only true variety shows are the specials presided over by Bob Hope, who has been on the tube since its inception, George Burns, and Dean Martin's occasional revival of his "Roasts." Occasionally, other stars do a one-hour variety show.

Variety will come back, it always does. Until recently, it was with us in a different guise. *Foul-Ups, Bleeps, and Blunders, TV's Bloopers and Practical Jokes,* and other programs similar in nature are technically variety shows. *Saturday Night Live,* though not in primetime, is currently continuing as one of the longest-running variety shows.

While the monetary rewards are great, there is also another major motivation in creating comedy. Probably no other occupation can be so enjoyable.

Writing humor and trying to make people laugh is something I have been doing since elementary school. When I was eleven my teacher told me I was one of the funniest kids she ever met. Also the dumbest. Comedy—I learned quickly—was a way of dealing with life. Although I am currently past the allotted biblical life span of three score and ten years, I hope to continue my career for many more. I'd like to emulate the English humorist, P. G. Wodehouse, who gave us the immortal character of Jeeves, and who even well past his eighties continued to publish at least one novel a year. On his ninety-fourth birthday he was interviewed and asked, "How can a ninety-four-year-old man consistently write such funny books?" Wodehouse is purported to have replied, "When I sit down to write, I'm twenty-five. When I take a three-mile hike I'm ninety-four."

That's the way I feel. When I'm writing comedy, I'm only twenty-five. Comedy has not only been my little gold mine, it's also my fountain of youth. Yes, writing it pays well, and making people laugh makes you feel young. And I often laugh because I can think of no happier business to be involved in.

COMEDY WRITING

I
THE ELEMENTS
OF HUMOR

Jokes

Writing comedy isn't so different from writing love stories or just about any other type of literature. You need to have real characters, sharp dialogue, true-to-life situations, a good sense of pace, balance, development—and once you have those ingredients, all you need to add is humor. There are many books available on the art of writing—books that will attempt to help you write strong dialogue or give your composition structure. I'll have a little to say on these things, but I'll be talking more about the unique business of writing comedy in television. As examples I will quote from some of the greatest scripts that have made millions of people laugh.

Jokes, per se, are the cheapest commodity in comedy. And the most necessary. But successful comedy is built around solid characters interacting in humorous situations, not just jokes. Every successful comedy series is peopled with characters you can identify with to some degree. The jokes have been fitted specifically to the person, which helps you identify with the character.

Basically, all jokes are constructed the same way. There is the feedline, then the punchline. The feedline sets the joke up, the punchline is the snapper that gets the laugh. This is true visually as well as vocally. For instance, when somebody throws a pie at the comedian, this is the feedline. When the comedian ducks and a third party (either an innocent bystander or somebody's boss) unexpectedly gets the pie in the face, that's the punchline. When either Bob Newhart or Shelley Berman does one of his famed telephone routines, he furnishes his own feed and punchlines by repeating what the invisible person on the phone has said to him.

The feedline, implied or stated, is just as important to the joke as the punchline. When the late John Tackaberry and I came up with what is supposedly Jack Benny's most famous joke, the feedline actually wrote itself. While walking one night, Jack was accosted by a holdup man who pulled a gun on him, and what was more natural for the crook to say than, "Your money or your life?" With Jack's long-time legendary reputation as a penny pincher we knew that Benny could just stare at the audience, and we'd get a huge laugh. But we needed a punch worthy of that feedline and it took us several hours and dozens of not quite good enough answers to have the crook repeat, "You heard me, your money or your life." And Jack screamed, "I'm thinking it over."

Some feedlines have more than one answer. There was a stag gag that made the rounds shortly after the astronauts took their giant step on the moon. It has two punchlines, and both are equally funny. Judge for yourselves.

The United States sent the first mixed team of astronauts, a man and woman, to visit Mars. They arrive on Mars and are greeted as guests and shown all over that planet. Finally they are taken to the Baby Making Room. They are amazed to see a group of workers gathered along a conveyor belt where one Martian places a lump of clay, another attaches two legs to the lump, and a third Martian sticks on two arms in the proper places. Then a head is added as the body moves and nose, ears, mouth, teeth, lips and eyes are added to the head. At the end of the assembly line the last Martian gives this creation an electric shock, and it becomes a living baby.

The earthman and woman express their amazement at this peculiar method of procreation. The Martians are surprised that Earthlings don't make babies via an assembly line like Martians, and ask how babies are made on our planet. In the interest of science the man and woman show them. They perform the entire sexual act, and now it is the Martians' turn to be surprised.

"That's amazing," says the head Martian. "That's the way we make automobiles."

The second snapper went as follows: The joke was told exactly the same way winding up with the man and woman having intercourse to show how babies are made on earth. When they finish, the Martians are puzzled and ask the couple, "But where's the baby?"

The man answers, "Oh, the baby won't be here for nine months."

"Nine months?" asks the Martian. "Then how come you were in such a hurry at the end?"

Many a movie, and TV episode, has based its entire plot on a single simple anecdote. One told how a golfer found a gorilla and taught it how to swing a golf club. The gorilla learned quickly and soon was hitting the ball tremendous distances. The man now bought the gorilla golf slacks and shirts, and took him to his club. He then made a thousand dollar bet with the pro at the club that he could bring out a golfer who had never played the game before and yet this golfer would beat the pro. The match was made. The first hole was a long one, 550 yards. The pro teed off first and hit a tremendous drive, 280 yards. The gorilla stepped up to the tee, took his driver, and hit the ball 550 yards so that it landed on the green—a feat that could not be duplicated by anyone from Ben Hogan to Jack Nicklaus. The crowd cheered and walked up the first fairway to where the pro's ball lay. The pro then hit another tremendous shot landing his ball on the green. They walked up to the green. The pro's ball was "away" (further from the pin). He therefore putted first and sunk his twenty-foot putt for an "eagle" three—two strokes less than par. Now it was the gorilla's turn to putt. His ball lay five feet from the hole, and if he sank it, he would have a double eagle two. (The double eagle is the most difficult achievement in golf—far rarer than a hole-in-one, which is merely an eagle.) The crowd hushed as the gorilla was handed his putter, and it waited to see the gorilla sink this short putt. The gorilla swung the putter and hit the ball another 550 yards.

That was the story, and it enjoyed great popularity among golfers. At that time Jim Backus was starring in a syndicated comedy series titled *Hot off the Wire*. Jim's wife, Henny Backus, a talented writer, took the joke, embroidered on it, worked the story so that famed golf pro Jimmy Demaret came on as a guest star and wound up in a match with the gorilla, and an amusing episode was the result.

Jokes are not only the basis for comedy but for dramatic shows as well. Some years ago a popular anecdote was told about an elderly man with many stocks in his portfolio. He was positive that in time their prices would reach astronomical figures, but he realized he was too old to see that day. Then he had an idea. He arranged for a scientist to freeze him so that he would sleep exactly one hundred years—and he left instructions for his stockbrokers to have their successors call him when the century had passed. One hundred years later the man's phone rings. It's his broker. He asks, "What is General Motors selling for?" "Twelve thousand dollars a share," was the answer. "And how much is Commodore Computers?" he happily inquired. "Eighteen thousand dollars a share," the broker answered. In rapid succession came the following questions and answers: "Polaroid?" "Six thousand five hundred dollars." "Xerox?" "Sixteen thousand dollars." "IBM?" "Twenty-two thousand dollars." The man, delirious with joy, asked, "And what's Ford Motors?" "Eight thousand dollars a share." And at this point the operator's voice cut in and said, "Your three minutes are up. Please deposit another ten thousand dollars."

That joke was very popular, especially with the Wall Street

set. It was also popular with an enterprising writer who some months later wrote a script that he sold to, I believe, *The Twilight Zone.* In this story a gang of crooks rob a Fort Knox type place and make off with several tons of gold. They hide it in a cave and take a drug that will put them to sleep for 100 years, figuring that the police won't be looking for them then. When they wake up a hundred years later, they emerge from the cave and are shocked to see that the roads are paved with gold, telephone poles are made of gold, and the once precious metal is now the commonest commodity in the world.

You see, a simple idea can occasionally be turned into a profitable script.

For practice purposes try writing jokes based on old comedy clichés. Feedlines that were once the staple of practically every standup comic but today are considered camp. Corny they may be but they are good enough to do your homework on. Here are some sample starters with snappers that actually did provoke guffaws not too long ago.

"My girl is so fat that . . . when she sits around the house, she sits around the house . . . when she turns around in the classroom, she erases all the blackboards."

"My girl has such big buck teeth . . . she can eat an apple through a picket fence . . . the Philharmonic uses her for a xylophone."

"My wife . . . talks so much, every time she goes to the beach her tongue gets sunburned . . . is so neat—once I got up at three in the morning to go to the bathroom, when I came back my bed was made . . . has a black belt in shopping."

"We were so poor . . . I wasn't born, I was made in Japan . . . we baited our mouse trap with a picture of cheese. The first night we caught a picture of a mouse."

"My hotel room . . . was so small, I had to go outside to change my mind . . . was so small, the mice were humpbacked . . . had such big fluffy towels, when I left I could hardly close my suitcase."

"It was so windy that . . . I saw a hen lay the same egg six times . . . I passed my house three times, and it passed me twice."

"It was so hot that . . . the tongues in the delicatessen windows were panting . . . I saw a dog chasing a cat, and they were both walking."

Oddly enough, one of the brightest, most sophisticated performers today, Johnny Carson, uses jokes of this type, but Johnny is smart enough to do it in a campy style. During the rainy season Johnny may say to the audience, "Gosh it was rainy today." And the audience, trained like Pavlov's pooches, will ask as one, "How rainy was it?" And Carson will answer laughingly, "Well, my roof was leaking, and I finished the same bowl of soup three times." (Of course, Carson, who has a highly paid staff of the best writers in TV, will have a better and newer answer than that.)

Make up your own feedlines. You can base them on anything. The long lines in supermarkets. Income taxes. Politics. Inflation. Traffic jams. Anything. But, as the old wheeze goes about the man who was lost on his way to a concert given by a famed pianist: He stopped and asked another man, "How do I get to Carnegie Hall?" And the answer was "Practice!"

Puns

The pun is the lowest form of humor. It is also one of the oldest devices used in literature. Is our humor too sophisticated today for use of the lowly pun?

No. There are good puns and bad puns, although sometimes the bad puns are good and vice versa. They can make an audience laugh and applaud, or groan and moan.

One of television's better and smarter programs, *Cheers,* occasionally uses puns to promote plot and character and to get laughs. And they get big ones. In one episode, Ted Danson (Sam) asked Shelley Long (Diane) how things were going with her in the romance department. She answered, "My love life is stable, and yours belongs in one." Pun one.

Later, the same episode, Ted is alone and accidentally shoots himself in the fanny. When Shelley learns about this, she solicitously asks him if he went to a doctor. He assures her he did, and she sweetly asks, "Did the doctor get the lead out?" Second pun.

Then Ted pleads with Shelley not to tell the rest of the bar's habitués that he shot himself in the fanny, and she answers, "I understand. You don't want to be the butt of their jokes." Third pun, third big laugh. (Shelley laughed politely to cover over the insensitivity of her last pun, which made it even funnier.)

The night prior to this program, Johnny Carson, in his monologue, mentioned a news story that said the Navy had paid $660 each for ashtrays, and that some months earlier the Pentagon had paid over $800 each for toilet seats. Then Johnny punned, "I guess the price depends on where you want to put your butt." A scream and applause.

Puns are often a scripter's standby today as they were over forty years ago during my days on the Bob Hope radio show. I remember a classic in construction and audience reception that we did during World War II, when almost everybody in California was working for defense plants, airplane manufacturers, or shipbuilders. It was our Halloween show, and we had Hope hiding in a haunted house. The lady who lived there informed Bob that her two brothers, Mel and Mort, worked as "riggers" in a shipyard, and that Mel got four dollars an hour but Mort received eight dollars an hour. Hope asked, "How come Mel doesn't make as much money as Mort?" And in a spooky voice she answered, "Because Mel is not the rigger Mort is." Yes, it was hokey and corny, but it was reprinted in many columns as the best joke of the week.

So don't scorn puns. Sure they're simple, but when they work, they work.

Malapropism

A close comedic cousin to the pun is the malapropism. The malapropism got its name from the character Mrs. Malaprop, in Richard Sheridan's play, *The Rivals,* written in 1775. Mrs. Malaprop mangled and mispronounced the vocabulary so horrendously that malapropism has become part of the English language to describe a word used incorrectly or incongruously.

Usually, a malapropism is a word that sounds almost like the intended one.

We have all heard malapropisms since childhood, and children sometimes come up with hilarious ones. I remember as a schoolboy hearing a funny pledge of allegiance to the flag. "I pledge allegiance to the flag and to the Republic for Richard Stands." Some fifty years later, this same joke was used in a Dennis the Menace cartoon. Whether it was intended as a joke when I first heard it, I know not. I do know that many children do this same line today, which is still another quarter of a century later.

Two of the funniest malapropisms I ever heard (actually read in a magazine) were also uttered by children. The first was a movie producer's child who said, "Our Father who art in Heaven, Hollywood be thy name." The second came from a New York tyke who in saying his prayers recited the immortal line, ". . . and lead us not into Penn Station." For years I wondered what the reaction of this kid would be if his parents took him on a train trip and led him into Penn Station. And on the subject of religion a six-year-old girl came home from church saying the congregation sang her favorite hymn, "Gladly, the Cross-Eyed Bear."

During the early days of broadcasting, when ethnic humor was quite acceptable, two popular characters were Yiddish accented, and they tended to Judaize everything. They were Fred Allen's Mrs. Nussbaum, whose favorite radio show was

Lum and Adler, and her favorite Broadway play was *The Lady's not For Bernstein.* Jack Benny's Mr. Kitzle said his favorite singers were Frank Sinatra, Bing Crosby, and Nat "King" Cohen. His favorite old-time baseball players were Tris Speaker, Babe Ruth, and Rabbi Maranville. (There was a famed baseball player named Rabbit Maranville.)

The most consistent user of malaprops in TV's history was Archie Bunker. These usually came from Archie's know-it-all attitude plus the audience's knowledge that he knew less than anyone else on the show. Or anywhere else. Archie didn't only mangle the English language, he frequently disemboweled it. And to make matters worse (or better as far as getting laughs), he was usually wrong at the top of his voice. One running gag was when Archie was losing an argument with anyone, which was the rule rather than the exception, he would put an end to the discussion by bellowing, "Case closed, ipso fatso."

We used at least one, and sometimes as many as four malapropisms on each program, and they usually paid off.

What really makes a malapropism work is how close to the real truth they are. On one episode Edith was going through the change of life, and Archie explained to Mike and Gloria, "She's going through mental pause." Then he suggested that Edith see a doctor specializing in female ailments, a "groinocologist." When he reacted too quickly to something, he said, "I just did it on the sperm of the moment." His explanation of the difference between men and women is that men have stronger sexual surges. When the police informed the Bunkers that they had captured a suspect who they thought was the man who tried to rape Edith, Archie pleaded, "Give me a knife and let me have five minutes alone with that guy, I'll make a unique out of him." And he claimed that his favorite TV comedy was *Levine and Shirley.*

A few of these the censors would not let us air. Archie was complaining that TV comics couldn't do any jokes about minorities because they all had organizations. "Tell jokes about blacks," he said, "they get the NACPPP after you. Tell a joke about Italians, and they call the Pope or they go over his head to Hoboken and get Frank Sinatra to take care of you. And if you tell a joke about Jews you get hell from the Anti-Defecation League."

And another notable no-no occurred during a show where Mike was in competition with a black teacher for a job as associate professor at a college in Minnesota. Archie, eager to keep his daughter and grandchild in Queens, next door to his house, does a role reversal and begins hoping for the black to beat the Meathead out for the job. When Mike wonders why Archie has turned pro-black, Bunker defends himself by saying, "I've never been against blacks. If I had my way every black in New York would be sent to Minnesota. . . . The blacks deserve a break—too long have they been low man on the scrotum pole." We were permitted to do the line about sending all the blacks in New York to Minnesota, but the line about "low man on the scrotum pole" was verboten.

The malapropism was a running reliable standby on *All in the Family.* There are some writers who feel that this device can be overdone. Maybe. However, I wouldn't want to argue the point with the highly successful comedian Norm Crosby, who for many years has garnered big boffs and bucks with routines composed almost exclusively of malapropisms.

The Play on Words

Slightly more difficult to write than puns and malapropisms is humor that depends on a play on words. Some of these get easy laughs because they sound funny. But not all.

The classic examples of the humor in playing on words comes mostly from skillfully constructed routines that have a central theme. One of the simplest examples of this, which became a running gag on Jack Benny's radio and TV shows for years, is Jack's meeting with Mel Blanc who played the Little Mexican. Because it has been reprinted frequently and clips of various segments still appear on TV, I'll give just a short sample here. The scene, a railroad station. Jack approaches Mel and speaks:

JACK

Excuse me, are you waiting for the train?

MEL

Si.

JACK

You're meeting someone on the train?

MEL

Si.

JACK

A relative?

MEL

Si.

JACK

What's your name?

MEL

Cy.

                              JACK

    Cy?

                              MEL

(FAST)

    Si.

                              JACK

    This relative you're waiting for, is it a woman?

                              MEL

    Si.

                              JACK

    What's her name?

                              MEL

    Sue.

                              JACK

    Sue?

                              MEL

    Si.

And so forth, on and on and on.
    Jack Benny's writers, Sam Perrin, George Balzer, John

Tackaberry, and I (later augmented by Hal Goldman and Al Gordon) did numerous versions of this routine.

Possibly the best known comedic play on words is Abott and Costello's justly famed "Who's on First" routine. They've both been gone many years, but you can hear kids and teenagers occasionally doing versions of "Who's on First?" with the use of "What? How? Where? Why?" It's a joy to watch Costello's growing exasperation at Abbott's calm explanations, and the sketch usually reduces the most critical viewer to a helpless laughing heap.

This comedy classic was copied numerous times with varying success until Johnny Carson did a takeoff enacting President Ronald Reagan readying himself for a press conference. It's very title, "Who's on First with President Reagan," admits it's a clone, but the fact that his audience was so familiar with the original may have helped it succeed so well that writers, usually niggardly in complimenting competitor's efforts, are unanimous in lavishing praise on it. It has already been repeated on Johnny's annual anniversary show and will probably be shown many more times.

It was written by head writer Raymond Siller, Kevin Mulholland, Gary Murphy, and Carson himself. Here's the routine as aired:

WHO'S ON FIRST WITH RONALD REAGAN

ED (SET-UP AT DESK)

> In President Reagan's last three or four press conferences, there has been criticism that the President was a little off in his facts. Some have suggested that the problem was due to inadequate briefing of the President by his staff members.

To see whether or not this is true, let's go to the Oval Office and listen in on one of these briefing sessions.

(CUT TO OVAL OFFICE SET)

(MUSIC: "HAIL TO THE CHIEF")

(JOHNNY ENTERS AS PRESIDENT RONALD REAGAN. WEARS BLUE SUIT. CROSSES TO DESK AND PRESSES INTERCOM.)

JOHNNY

Would you send in Jim Baker?

(ADVISER ENTERS AND JOHNNY JOINS HIM DOWNSTAGE IN FRONT OF DESK.)

ADVISER

Mr. President, your press conference is scheduled one hour from now so we only have a short time to brief you on some of the questions the reporters may throw at you.

JOHNNY

Well, the environment is on their minds. I'm sure they'll ask me about my Secretary of the Interior.

ADVISER

Watt.

JOHNNY

I said I'm sure they'll ask me about my Secretary of the Interior.

ADVISER

Watt.

JOHNNY

I just told you they'll ask me about my Secretary of the Interior.

ADVISER

James Watt. You're scheduled to swim with him tomorrow morning at the Y.

JOHNNY

Where?

ADVISER

Y.

JOHNNY

Why?

ADVISER

That's right. With Watt.

JOHNNY

With what? I don't even know with who.

ADVISER

Not who . . . Watt.

JOHNNY

Let me get this straight. I'm going swimming tomorrow with who?

ADVISER

Watt.

JOHNNY

Where?

ADVISER

Y.

JOHNNY

Let's go to the Middle East. I need the first name of the head of the PLO . . . that Arafat guy.

ADVISER

Yassir.

JOHNNY

I said I need the first name of the head of the PLO.

ADVISER

Yassir.

JOHNNY

Look, it's nice that you're polite, but what is his name?

ADVISER

No sir . . . Yassir.

JOHNNY

You're giving me two different answers, Jim. What is his name?

ADVISER

No sir . . . Yassir.

JOHNNY

I ask you the first name of the head of the PLO. You tell me "No sir."

ADVISER

That's right.

JOHNNY

Then you tell me "Yes sir."

ADVISER

Absolutely. You got it.

JOHNNY

I got what?

ADVISER

He's your Secretary of the Interior.

JOHNNY

Why are you doing this to me?

(SFX: PHONE RINGS)
(ADVISER PICKS UP PHONE. JOHNNY IS MUMBLING TO HIMSELF.)

ADVISER

(INTO PHONE)

Hello . . . You have the head of the Republic of China
on the line . . . Premier Chung Dung Hu.

(HANDING JOHNNY PHONE)

Mr. President, Hu's on the line.

JOHNNY

I don't know. Who's on the line?

ADVISER

That's correct.

JOHNNY

What's correct?

ADVISER

No, he's your Secretary of the Interior.

JOHNNY

Let's start all over again. Who's the head of the PLO.?

ADVISER

No sir . . . Yassir. Hu's on the line.

JOHNNY

What?

ADVISER

Tomorrow morning at the Y.

(CUT TO CLOSE UP OF JOHNNY WITH "NO MORE . . . PLEASE!" LOOK ON FACE.)
(MUSIC: "HAIL TO THE CHIEF" PLAYOFF)
(APPLAUSE)
(FADE OUT)

The movies have always come up with fantastically funny scenes depending on playing on words. To me though, the funniest occurred in *The Court Jester,* starring Danny Kaye. It was written, directed and produced by the team of Norman Panama and Mel Frank.

It's legendary among writers, and I've worked with many who weren't born when the picture was released in 1952, yet they can repeat it verbatim. Here is a condensed version of the routine.

Danny, as Hawkins, must do battle with a feared knight, Grisly Grimwald. Griselda, a witchlike woman, tells Danny he has nothing to fear because she has doctored the drinks the combatants will toast with.

GRISELDA

Listen. I've put a pellet of poison in one of the vessels.

HAWKINS

Which one?

GRISELDA

The one with the figure of a pestle.

HAWKINS

The vessel with the pestle?

GRISELDA

Yes. But you don't want the vessel with the pestle, you want the chalice from the palace.

HAWKINS

I see. I want a chalice from the—what?

JEAN
(impatiently)

The chalice from the palace.

HAWKINS

Hmm?

GRISELDA
(rapidly)

A little crystal chalice with a figure of a palace.

HAWKINS
(quickly)

But does the chalice with the palace have the pellet with the poison?

GRISELDA

No, the pellet with the poison's in the vessel with the pestle.

HAWKINS

The pestle with the vessel?

JEAN

No—the vessel with the pestle!

HAWKINS

What about the palace from the chalice?

GRISELDA
(sternly)

Not the palace from the chalice, the *chalice* from the *palace!*

HAWKINS

And where's the pellet with the poison?

GRISELDA

In the vessel with the pestle.

JEAN
(impatiently)

Don't you see—
(rapidly)
The pellet with the poison's in the vessel with the pestle, the chalice from the palace has the brew that is true! It's so simple. *I* can say it.

HAWKINS

Then *you* fight him.

GRISELDA
(enunciating slowly)

Now listen carefully. The pellet with the poison's in the vessel with the pestle, the chalice from the palace has the brew that is true.

HAWKINS
(he's got it)

The pellet with the poison's in the vessel with
the pestle, the chalice from the palace has the
brew that is true.

JEAN

Good man.

GRISELDA

Just remember that.

[GRISELDA LEAVES HAWKINS (DANNY) WHO KEEPS REPEATING
VARIOUS SCREWED UP VERSIONS OF "THE VESSEL WITH THE PES-
TLE AND THE CHALICE FROM THE PALACE." FINALLY HE AP-
PROACHES GRISELDA TRIUMPHANTLY.]

HAWKINS

I've got it!
(quickly)
The pellet with the poison's in the vessel with
the pestle, the chalice from the palace has the
brew that is true! Right?

GRISELDA
(frantically)

No, no, there's been a change.

HAWKINS

What???

                    GRISELDA
They broke the chalice from the palace.

                    HAWKINS
Oh, no!

                    GRISELDA
And replaced it with a flagon.

                    HAWKINS
A flagon??

                    GRISELDA
With a figure of a dragon.

                    HAWKINS
                  (memorizing)
The flagon with the dragon.

                    GRISELDA
Right.

GRISWOLD'S AIDE PASSES BY, STOPS, REACTS AS HE HEARS:

                    HAWKINS
                  (rapid fire)
But did you put the pellet with the poison in
the vessel with the pestle?

GRISELDA
(quickly)

No. The pellet with the poison's in the flagon
with the dragon, the vessel with the pestle has
the brew that is true.

HAWKINS

Oh, I see.
(rapidly)
The pellet with the poison's in the flagon with
the dragon, the vessel with the pestle has the
brew that is true!

Griswold's aide hurries off and informs Griswold of the
mickey finn and where it is. The payoff comes when Hawkins
and Griswold approach each other to fight, each repeating
their own laughable versions of "Vessel with the pestle and
flagon with the dragon."

You've now read some superb samples of playing with
words. Try to write similar routines, but don't be discouraged
if you don't succeed. It took many topflight writers several
decades to come up with those you've just read.

Monologues

The simplest form of comedy writing, and yet one of the most
lucrative for the performer and writer, is the monologue. Basically, a monologue is several jokes strung together and usually dealing with one subject. Practically every comedian and
comedienne on the tube today started via the humble monologue and still uses this device as a stable stock in trade, and
most writers started their careers the same way.

Bob Hope began to skyrocket to fame in 1938 with his topical monologues. Through many years, Bob has started every one of his weekly radio shows and all his television specials with a monologue, making humorous comments on current events. Bob wasn't the first one to do this. Will Rogers started as a lasso twirling cowboy, but his caustic cracks about the state of the country and the world made his reputation. Comic monologues date back to Roman times.

In the days of radio and early television, when shows were done live, almost all monologues were on topical subjects. With the advent of taped and filmed shows, there are few who do topical material, a loss to the listeners in my opinion. Johnny Carson opens every show with a monologue that is as fresh as the daily newspaper. True, not all the jokes in his routines play, but at least you know that he is jesting about something that just happened. Enough of his gags click to make his openings the highlight of my TV viewing. And even when an occasional joke falls flat, Johnny has an ad-lib to make it worthwhile. He takes a chance on untried material, and much more often than not it pays off for him.

Bob Hope now films his specials well in advance—except for his monologue. He usually waits for a day or two prior to his program's air date before doing his opening. Hope will usually take two or three topical subjects and rapid-fires his goodies at a live audience. Because Bob tapes his monologues, he has the luxury of deleting those lines that seem less appreciated by his audience.

When Hope or Carson does a monologue, you immediately recognize it as such because it is the standard form. But there are numerous popular monologists whose routines don't seem like monologues, yet they are. For instance, Red Buttons has developed a unique technique. When a celebrity is honored on a TV Roast or other function, Red does a routine citing all the people in history who were never so honored. On Bob Hope's "Birthday Special" on May 28, 1984, Red said lines like: "And

Adam . . . Adam who said to God, I've got more ribs, have You got more broads—never had a party." The following night Buttons appeared on *Foul-Ups, Bleeps, and Blunders* and said, "John Travolta—who made *Saturday Night Fever* and then got a Sunday morning rash—never had a bleep."

Rodney Dangerfield's monologues are all based on his claim, "I don't get no respect. Even my twin brother forgets my birthday." Phyllis Diller jokes about her looks. "I was in the beauty parlor ten hours yesterday and that was just for an estimate." George Burns targets his age as did Jack Benny, who stayed thirty-nine for decades. Burns once said, "When I was eighty-six, an insurance doctor asked me, 'When did sex stop for you?' and I told him—'At three o'clock this morning.' I passed the exam." Joan Rivers takes potshots at everyone. When Elizabeth Taylor was very overweight, Joan said, "Liz had her ears pierced, and they hit gravy. Her thighs are going condo."

Stand-up comics try to get audiences to love them, but not Don Rickles, who insults everyone and earned the nickname "The Merchant of Venom." And Henny Youngman is an exception to the rule that all monologues should be on the same subject, preferably with a point of view or attitude. When Henny started many years ago, he didn't bother to aim his witticisms at any particular subject but scattered his jibes at everything and anything, jumping from subject to subject like a grasshopper. A typical Youngman routine might go something like this: "My brother went to a psychiatrist and said, 'Doctor, my trouble is that everybody ignores me,' and the psychiatrist said, 'Next.' . . . Which reminds me, my wife phoned and said, "I think I have water in my carburetor." I asked, "Where's your car?" She said, "In the swimming pool." . . . By the way, I played golf in Miami in the eighties. That was the temperature, not my score."

Henny doesn't carefully build his routine on a subject, milking it for all the possible laughs. Instead, he shoots his jokes out rapid-fire and willy-nilly. Some miss, some hit, but his hits are so numerous and unexpected you don't mind the misses.

Many talk about their childhood and ethnic upbringing. Gary Shandlin, David Steinberg, David Brenner give us Jewish jokes, as does Buddy Hackett who oddly enough scored his first big hit doing a monologue-type routine as a Chinese waiter. Pat Cooper talks about his Italian heritage. Blacks do jokes about their problems. Dick Gregory was known for bitter funny truths like, "A black man pays $60,000 for a $20,000 house in a white neighborhood, and then everybody is mad at him because he's lowering real estate values."

Many comedians reminisce about their families and childhood. The late Sam Levinson's entire repertoire was based on this. Wives talk about husbands, and vice versa. Most of Bill Cosby's recent late night and concert appearances devote much time to his children and his 1986 book, *Fatherhood,* which became an almost instant number one best-seller.

Norm Crosby does routines where jokes are almost always malapropisms. Alan King aims his barbs at the establishment, including doctors, lawyers, airlines, and apartment house doormen and other attendants who suddenly switch from surly to sweet two weeks before Christmas. Mort Sahl's prop is a newspaper, and he comments on the various items that strike his fancy. His nightclub act features the same bit, and much of his act is different every night.

The forms in which you can write monologues are numerous. George Jessel used to do one-way telephone calls with his mother. Shelley Berman used the telephone device. Lily Tomlin's big break came as Ernestine, the nasal telephone operator on *Laugh-In.* Bob Newhart broke into the business with hugely successful records in which he held imaginary phone conversations with such long-dead celebrities as the Wright Brothers, ridiculing their newly invented airplane, or Sir Walter Raleigh where Newhart wants to know what you do with the strange plant he had discovered the Indians using in the new world. It went something like this: "Tobacco? . . . they cut it up and put it in tubes? And then they *what? Smoke* it? Ha ha ha." The one-way telephone monologue has always been an excellent device since the preradio days in the early twenties when possibly the first comedy record, "Cohen on the Telephone," became a big seller. He was talking to his landlord and said, "This is your new tenant, Cohen . . . Your new tenant Cohen . . . No, not Lieutenant Cohen."

Certain performers' monologues are usually short, dramatic pieces done as anecdotes. Jack Benny's favorite routine on talk shows, specials, and nightclubs told how he picked up a beautiful girl in Las Vegas, and she took him to her hotel room. They danced, and she asked Jack if he'd like to kiss her, and Jack said yes. The girl then said, "Well first I'll have to take off my wig." Jack asked, "Take off your wig?" And the girl said, "Yes, I'm Allen Funt and you're on *Candid Camera.*" The routine ran anywhere from five to eight minutes getting good laughs, building to a solid payoff because it was all tailored to Benny's character.

The acknowledged master at turning an anecdote into a monologue is Danny Thomas. Some of his gems include the tribulations of a Jewish man who buys a parrot that can chant Hebraic prayers, buys it a small prayer shawl and yarmulke and tries to take it into the synagogue on the High Holy Days. Another deals with an Italian making a telephone call from a very warm booth, and keeps complaining, "It's a hot in da boots." And his best known is his "jack" story.

Danny tells of a man who is walking to a friend's house to borrow a jack, which he needs for auto repairs. As he walks, he begins to worry that he might be turned down. To bolster his spirits he recalls favors he had done for this friend. Then he answers each favor with further reasons why his friend will reject him. The longer he walks, the more reasons, and then rejections, he thinks of. And he is getting tireder and angrier. When he reaches his friend's door and rings the bell, the friend opens the door, smiles and says, "Danny, it's good to see you." Danny snarls, "Oh, yeah, you can take your damned jack and shove it."

Before dropping this subject, it should be pointed out that frequently a good monologue joke can be dished up as dialogue. If you analyze some of the routines on the Cosby comedy series, you will come to the conclusion that an occasional hysterical bit probably started as one of his famed monologues, and by having other characters interject questions or lines, it has become blended into the very funny dialogue you hear on the program.

Every writer realizes that good monologue jokes are easily converted into dialogue—and dialogue is the most important ingredient in situation comedies.

II
Tricks of the Trade

Toilers in every occupation have, through years of experience, learned so-called tricks of the trade and techniques to make their jobs simpler and more successful.

Bartenders sometimes water their drinks, butchers are accused of weighing their thumbs along with their steaks, painters may give your kitchen one coat of paint and charge you for two, no one knows what plumbers do, and I won't discuss used car salesmen at all.

All of the aforementioned examples range from unethical to downright dishonest, but no such taint besmirches the various shortcuts, formulas, and devices developed by those who earn their daily bread and Perrier with the sweat of their typewriters. They are all honorable and worthwhile. Many of them should be included in every writer's bible. What follows is a potpourri of suggestions, which are sometimes obvious to tyros but occasionally only acquired via experience. Here they are:

Brevity

Too many jokes are hurt by adding extra words. The amateur humorist, either through ignorance or confidence that he can improve the jest, tacks on superfluous syllables and words.

Here's an example: A rabbi received a phone call at his temple from a man from the Internal Revenue Service and their conversation was as follows:

MAN FROM IRS

Rabbi, do you know a man named Hyman Shapiro?

RABBI

I do.

MAN FROM IRS

Does he belong to your temple?

RABBI

He does.

MAN FROM IRS

Did he make a $10,000 donation to your temple?

RABBI

He will.

Told this way, the joke has perfect rhythm and not one superfluous syllable. But I heard one man tell it with a slightly different punchline. He had the rabbi answer, "No, but he will." The addition of the two words, "No, but" hurt rather than helped the story.

An even more egregious example occurred some years ago when a guest on a talk show gave his version of Jack Benny's most famous gag. He related it fairly well except that when the holdup man said to Jack, "Your money or your life?," he had Benny answer, "Just give me a minute, I'm thinking it over." The addition of those front five words ruined the rhythm, made the joke longer, and watered it down.

Rhythm

Jokes and routines are helped by rhythm. Milton Berle and his writers were once discussing the importance of cadence in comedy. Berle said he would conduct an experiment. When he finished that week's broadcast, he would do a monologue for the studio audience. He would start by doing three jokes, all proved funny via past performances, and all having the same exact rhythm. Then he would do a fourth joke in the same exact rhythm, but the punchline would be a nonsensical non-sequitur; and it would still get a laugh. It went exactly as Berle had predicted. True, the fourth and pointless gag did not get as big a reception as the ones it succeeded, but it got a respectable response.

Rhyme

For some reason a weak or corny line will pay off much bigger if done in rhyme. Jack Benny's violin teacher, Professor Le-Blanc (Mel Blanc), would keep the beat as Jack practiced with jingles like:

> Make the bow strokes a little longer.
> How I wish my stomach were stronger.

On one sitcom when the entire cast became overexcited, an actress took charge with the line: "Don't panic, keep calm.

Remember the immortal words of Marie Antoinette who observed, 'Keep cool when all's done and said, Above all remember, don't lose your head.' "

Repetition

Sometimes repeating a single word, short phrase, or bit of business can build to a worthwhile climax. On numerous episodes *All in the Family* did routines where Archie would tell Edith something she didn't quite comprehend or believe. She would say "No?" with various intonations and Archie would answer "Yes" several times with different inflections and get guffaws on these single syllables. At other times Jean Stapleton, as Edith, would keep repeating the word "Oh" as something dawned on her, and she realized its meaning. Edith sometimes seemed to use this short interjection as a complete vocabulary. Her "Oh" could denote surprise, sympathy, skepticism, and satisfaction. With her delivery it became a verb, a question, an answer, and an expression of understanding, sorrow, or joy. Usually we tried to limit the usage to three or four successive "Ohs." However, we once did an episode where a woman who lived with Edith's recently deceased cousin explained to Edith that she was closer to the cousin than Edith —closer than a husband—and when it finally dawned on Edith that this woman and her cousin had a lesbian relationship, she gave vent to six or seven "Ohs," which ran the spectrum of emotion from comprehension to compassion. Each of her "Ohs" was greeted with excellent audience reaction and well-deserved applause at the end. Then later when Edith explained it to Archie, he got the same results by repeating the word "No."

The repetition of a funny sound is a guaranteed laugh getter. On an *AITF* episode Archie and Edith had argued and now were talking via intermediaries, Mike and Gloria. Finally, Archie blew up and told Mike, "Just tell her BIRD." And he gave vent to a loud juicy BIRD. (The BIRD, Bronx Cheer, or Lip Fart, is a rude but funny noise Archie frequently used to end his arguments.) Mike said, "I'm not going to tell her BIRD." Archie then ordered Gloria: "You tell her BIRD." Gloria responded, "I won't say BIRD to my mother." Archie: "Why not, you go BIRD to your father." Gloria: "I only go BIRD to my father when he goes BIRD to me." It doesn't read like much, but if you keep repeating it with the appropriate sound effects, it gets quite funny. And we topped the entire routine with a close-up shot of baby Joey giving vent to a loud juicy BIRD.

Role Reversal

This is a much-used almost always successful comedic gimmick. It is exactly what the words imply: Performers temporarily adopt character traits contrary to those they normally have. The most common is the gender switch, and in movies and TV it most frequently works best where a man portrays a woman. True, Julie Andrews got laughs going masculine in *Victor/Victoria,* and Lucille Ball posed as a man many times with excellent results.

On the other hand, Jack Lemmon and Tony Curtis were hilarious as members of an all-girl band in *Some Like It Hot.* The TV series *Bosom Buddies* had Peter Scolari and Tom Hanks dressed in drag. Milton Berle wore ladies' outfits so often that once he said he was disappointed that he wasn't picked as the best dressed woman of the year.

The movie *Mr. Mom* had the husband assuming the wifely chores while his spouse acted as the breadwinner. The current hit TV show *Who's the Boss?* has Tony Danza holding down a normally feminine job as housekeeper, and his boss is a lady executive.

A classic character role reversal occurred on *All in the Family* when Mike applies for an associate professorship at a Minnesota college but he has competition in his friend, John Kasten. John is black, and Mike is afraid he'll get the job because of reverse discrimination. Gloria accuses him of bigotry, and Mike indignantly insists he's no bigot. "I'd just hate to lose this job to John because he was lucky enough to be born black."

Conversely, Archie wants Kasten to get the job because if Mike goes to Minnesota so do Archie's beloved daughter and grandson. Archie turns liberal and gives the following declamation on Democracy:

"Lady Liberty is standing out there in the harbor with her torch held high, screaming out to all the nations of the world, 'Send me your poor, your deadbeats, your filthy. And all the nations sent them in here. They come crawling in like ants. Your Spanish PRs from the Carriboon, your Japs, your Chinamen, your Krauts, your Hebes, your English Fags. All of them come in here, and they're all free to live in their own separate sections where they feel safe, and they'll bust your head if you come in there. That's what makes America great, buddy.'"

Archie made his exit to laughter and applause, which was topped when Mike turned to Gloria and said, "I think we just heard Archie Bunker's Bicentennial Minute." (The episode was taped in 1976 when it seemed you watched a Bicentennial Minute every ten seconds.)

Sesquipedalianisms and Exoticisms

This is a polysyllabic means of saying fancy and foreign words. Usually, these should be avoided. What the audience doesn't understand it doesn't laugh at. Bob Hope once said, "I don't like traveling by boat because the ocean can get too rough, and I suffer from *mal-de-mer*. *Mal-de-mer*. That's

French for you can't take it with you." Even if the audience didn't know any foreign language, they got the idea that *mal-de-mer* meant seasick when he told the joke.

A surefire gambit is to have a very dignified performer use an unexpected word or expression. Example: The suave Academy Award winner Ronald Colman once lost patience with Jack Benny and in his British-accented tones yelled, "Why you —you—you *Shlemiel.*" (*Shlemiel* is Yiddish for simpleton, but the audience didn't have to understand because the word sounds funny.) Robin Williams, who was Mork from Ork, used to ad-lib many Yiddishisms, frequently referring to Mindy as "my favorite *shicksa.*" (*Shicksa* means a non-Jewish girl.) *Shicksa* has a "k" in it, and "k" words are supposedly funny. Telling someone "Go bite an apple" will not get as big a reaction as "Go suck a kumquat," which has a double "k" sound.

Corny Jokes

Don't be afraid to try something obviously hokey and corny if it fits perfectly into the situation. This is an exception, and not a rule, but writers have successfully inserted slapstick bits in sophisticated series. The one that sticks out in my memory was in an *All in the Family* script I wrote with Ben Starr, and it was Ben who literally forced me to put in the routine. It was during the several shows we did concerning Gloria's pregnancy when she was determined to have her baby via natural childbirth. And she was equally determined that a rather reluctant Mike would be in the delivery room when she gave birth. In this episode Archie kept harping on the fact that the delivery room was no place for any man. "That's why the doctors wear masks, because they don't want nobody to recognize them." Archie finally dissuades Mike, which infuriates Gloria, and she, preceded by her pregnant tummy, waddles out of the Bunker house to her home next door. Mike sheepishly follows her home, and she berates him while preparing an omelette for lunch. She says he probably doesn't even want the baby. Mike protests and says that he can't wait to become a father. Angrily Gloria puts an egg in Mike's hand and says, "You want a child? Here, hatch this."

Mike starts after her, but the doorbell rings, and he goes to it and admits Archie and Edith. Archie is gloating over his triumph and says, "Meathead, for once you done something sensible. I want to shake your hand," and he immediately grabs Mike's hand and shakes it vigorously, smashing the raw egg in their grip. Archie looks at the mess, then at Mike, then turns to Edith and says, "I swear, he's been walking around carrying that egg for five years waiting for me to shake hands with him."

When we read the routine at the first cast reading, someone said, looking at me, "That sounds more like the Lucille Ball show." Sheepishly I admitted it was my brainchild, and I could easily delete it. But Rob Reiner said, "It fits perfectly here," and Carroll loved it—and so did the audience.

Gimmicks

Because there is a dearth of good comedy gimmicks, certain stratagems are used endlessly. You know the clichés.

When the scene ends with the husband announcing to his wife in no uncertain terms, "Under no condition will I dress up in a monkey suit and go to that party," you can rely on the very next scene to show him at that party dressed in a tuxedo.

When the wife forces her reluctant husband to attend her twenty-fifth high-school class reunion, because she wants him to meet the handsome hunk, usually the quarterback on the football team, who was her teenaged boyfriend, just look around at the party and pick the fattest, baldest klutz—that's him.

When several adults are futilely struggling to remove the "child proof" cover on a bottle of pills and finally set it aside frustrated, you can bet the family jewels that the first six-year-old kid to enter the room will pick up the bottle and open it instantly.

When a character in a comedy picks up a bowling ball, that character is going to have it unremovably stuck to his hand for some time or the ball wouldn't have been in the scene in the first place. (Unless it's in a bowling alley, and then the character may slide down the alley with the ball.)

Clichés crop up in all comedy shows. The veteran writers use them occasionally but only where they fit the situation. Try to avoid them if you don't want your material to look hackneyed, but if you do use one, get a clever switch; it will be a credit to your script rather than a liability.

Doing, and Yet Not Doing, the Obvious

When the occasion arises for this gimmick, the punch is usually doubly appreciated. You start with a feed line or situation where the payoff is so obvious it's apparent to practically everyone in the audience. Then you double-cross them. The following setup, in diverse forms, pops up on programs, usually in a sketch on a variety show.

It starts with a well-endowed diva about to entertain with several arias, and one character says, "She has a rather large repertoire." The second character will look at the prima donna's ample posterior and then favor the camera with a knowing leering look and say something like, "I wouldn't touch a feedline like that with a ten-foot pole." Or "I refuse to ad-lib at that level." Whatever the line may be, it is always preceded by a rewarding laugh when the character stares at her rear end and then the audience is conditioned to laugh at whatever line is pulled, but try and make it one they don't expect.

A close cousin to the preceding is having the audience anticipate exactly what will happen but delaying it so it comes when they are lulled into believing it won't happen. Many shows do this successfully but it was carried out to an art on Lucille Ball's various series—especially her third one, *Here's Lucy*.

The first occasion I remember it being done was when Lucy, working in Gale Gordon's office, discovered that the huge bottle sitting on top of the water cooler seemed to be empty, and she struggled with the unwieldy container trying to remove it. From the early days of *I Love Lucy* through all the years she ruled the airwaves, audiences knew that when Lucy was in a situation like that, disaster would soon strike, and the viewers in our studio began to laugh knowing something was going to happen, but they knew not what.

Gale Gordon watched her unsuccessful joust with the unwieldy container and gallantly came to her aid. Very easily he lifted the bottle—only it wasn't quite empty and a couple of quarts cascaded down his pants. Several weeks later we did the reverse of this. Lucy removed the empty bottle with ease, and the laughing audience seemed disappointed when she didn't get soaked. However, when she tried to lift the full bottle replacement, it was much too heavy for her. So Gordon, with some strain, lifted it, but as he was about to invert it to install in the cooler, Lucy noticed that the cork or cover was over the bottle's mouth and naturally she had to remove it, and naturally the audience knew what was going to happen, and naturally Gale got soaked again.

I believe we used three or four variations on this device that year, and when the season ended and we had a little "wrap" party, Gale Gordon was given a gift. A wet jock strap, which represented "The Soggy Crotch of the Year Award."

Visual Humor

In the 1940s a magazine asked, "Who is the best known person in the entire world, living or dead, historical or mythical, or even religious?" Was it Jesus, Moses, Buddha, Mohammed, Franklin D. Roosevelt, Hitler, Churchill, or Stalin? No, the most identifiable person in the world was Charlie Chaplin (and this item appeared years after he stopped making movies). His renown didn't come from his later pictures like *Modern Times* or *The Great Dictator,* but his earlier silent shorts and features. The magazine item pointed out that each day over 15 to 20 million people around the world were watching Charlie's antics.

It didn't matter what country the shorts were shown in, or what language the subtitles were in. Everyone understands a pie in the face, and a pratfall is funny to all. Visual humor is universal.

In television today the comedy shows fare poorest when sold in the foreign market. Most of our shows are more verbal than visual and not comprehended by those who do not speak English. Even by some who do speak the language. A short time ago Johnny Carson's programs were broadcast in England, but soon dropped because they didn't understand his humor. Possibly it was too topical, or too local, or perhaps the English just don't understand our English.

I believe the comedy show that converted best into exotic tongues was *I Love Lucy* and her subsequent series. Miss Ball probably used more physical comedy than any other TV star. And her programs are shown in more countries than any other show. There wasn't anything she wouldn't do, or a risk she wouldn't take, a gimmick she wouldn't try to get laughs. In various episodes she blacked out her teeth, wore a GI close-cropped haircut, got herself completely covered with crushed grapes in a wine-stomping episode, crossed her eyes, made up as an exact replica of Harpo Marx. Countless times she was drenched with water from head to toe, had her face covered with whipped cream, tunafish, olives and peaches for a phony beauty treatment, and that wonderful scene when they were in Hollywood: Desi brought home her favorite movie star, William Holden, to meet Lucy, not knowing she had had an adjoining booth to his for lunch at the Brown Derby and, Lucylike, she had caused everything to be spilled on him, including getting hit in his face with a cream-covered cake. The one man she didn't want to meet at that time was William Holden.

So Lucy, hiding in her bedroom, grabbed Desi's movie makeup kit and put on a face that would have been envied by Lon Chaney. She topped it all off with a three-inch Cyrano de Bergerac beak. When she entered the living room in response to Desi's persistent calling, she took care that he didn't see her face. But Holden did and reacted. He didn't recognize her as the person who ruined his noontime meal, not to mention his clothes. He reacted to her as a weird-looking lady. Lucy tried to act nonchalant and put a cigarette in her mouth. Ever the gentleman, Holden took out his lighter and lighted Lucy's cigarette. He also lighted Lucy's nose, which began to go up in flames. She finally extinguished the fire by dunking her shish-kebabbed schnozz into a cup of coffee.

I learned of Lucy's love for action with the first script I worked on when I became her Script Consultant. It was written by Garry Marshall and Jerry Belson, and after we rewrote it, I took it to Lucy for her reaction. She flipped through the thirty-eight pages in what seemed seconds, then said, "It's going to be a good script, it's loaded with black stuff."

I nodded knowingly but hadn't the faintest idea what she meant. Then it dawned on me. Dialogue is written double-spaced. Stage directions, which indicate action, are single-spaced, all capital letters, and a page loaded with directions for physical action looks black.

Briefly, here is some of the "black stuff" in the script:

The entire episode was based on a premise that because of swollen feet after an afternoon skating with her daughter, Lucy went to a dance wearing the skates, covered by a long dress. She tried to make a dignified entrance, but someone pushed her, and she went speeding across the dance floor. Blocking her path was a large, food-laden table, and Lucy ducked and skated under it. Then she seemed destined to roll forever when she spotted a slender brass pole running from floor to ceiling. She hooked her arm around it, circled it rapidly several times, let go, and shot forward, crashing into her glaring boss, Mr. Mooney (Gale Gordon), and smiled at him demurely as though this was the proper way to enter a room.

The scene was long and difficult. Lucy did it in one take, the audience loved it, and I made sure all future scripts were loaded with "black stuff."

I remember one outstanding visual vignette that got huge laughs via action that seemed unplanned:

Jack Benny and Bob Hope were performing a sketch in which Jack Benny finds out that Hope is making time with his wife. Jack confronted the home wrecker, pulled out a pistol, pointed it at Bob, and said, "I'm going to blow your brains out." However, Benny wasn't pointing the pistol at Hope's head. It was, in fact, aimed at another part of Bob's anatomy. To be specific, the pistol was pointed at those parts of a man that, if he ain't got them, he ain't a man. Hope stared at Jack, then down where the weapon was aimed. Jack, rest his soul, was the easiest audience in the world. As Bob stared at the pistol's target, Jack broke up. Then Hope reached down and very, very slowly elevated the pistol till it was aimed at his head. Not a word was uttered, which is just as well because nothing could be heard above that pandemonium.

I have been in the business long enough to detect a well-rehearsed ad-lib, and there are plenty, but to this day I don't know whether that one was prepared in advance or a lucky accident.

So those are some visual bits, and all comedy writers, beginners or veterans, would do well to try to create new ones. But remember this—dialogue can also paint a vivid visual effect. In the days of radio many of Fred Allen's jests were actually pictures for the mind's eye. He had a character on his program named Titus Moody who spoke with a New England accent. One week they were discussing hunting and displaying the bagged animals in trophy rooms. Moody said, "Uncle of mine was a great hunter. Shot everything. Only he didn't stuff or mount the heads—just the other ends." Allen asked, "You mean he keeps the rear—" And Moody interrupted him by saying, "Yep, when you enter his den, you feel like you're overtaking a herd." Everytime I think of that joke, I feel that I'm watching a stampede run away from me.

Sometimes you can use offstage, unseen sound effects that will paint a clear visual picture. During the days of radio most of the programs had running gags that depended on sound effects. The most famous of these was probably Fibber McGee's overstuffed closet. All the audience had to hear was Fibber's fateful phrase, "I'll get it out of the closet," and they'd start laughing before the avalanche of junk came cascading to the floor. Jack Benny fans will never forget the sound of his famed Maxwell's motor coughing and sputtering (mostly supplied by the ubiquitous Mel Blanc) as it started. Another favorite ear piercer was the familiar sound of the burglar alarm as Benny opened his subterranean vault.

The offstage sound can be used for laughs with a little imagination. We once did a *Lucy* show where Lucy broke her leg, and Vivian Vance came to California from New York to nurse her pal. Lucy was confined to a bed with her leg in traction, and Vivian wanted to know what happened. Lucy sheepishly admitted that she tripped on a small hole in the kitchen linoleum. Viv thought this was funny—that after all the wild crazy stunts Lucy did without injury, she should get hurt over a simple thing like that. Lucy wanted a glass of water, and Viv went into the kitchen to get it. As she left, Lucy warned her,

"Look out for that hole in—" and the rest of the sentence was drowned by the sound of a body falling to the floor offstage. A surefire laugh provoker, and I'm positive we didn't invent this hilarity via unseen but clearly pictured shtick.

A wonderful "verbal visual" bit we did on *All in the Family* had sound effects to start the routine, and dialogue to end it.

Archie was holed up in the bathroom, and the ever reliable laugh-getting toilet was being flushed every thirty seconds. Then Archie yelled down plaintively, "Edith, I'm out of terlet paper, I need a fresh roll." There were several seconds of silence as the camera played on Edith's changing expressions as she thought about this. Then she called up, "Archie, you'll find a fresh roll in the cabinet to your right if you're standing, to your left if you're sitting." Another word picture painted quite graphically.

Juxtaposition

"Juxtaposition" as defined by the Oxford Universal Dictionary, means, "The action of placing two or more things close together or side by side; the condition of being so placed."

"Juxtaposition," as defined by comedy writers, means a tried and true technique of doing a routine bound to get surefire laughs because of misinterpretation. Juxtaposition has been used by Boccaccio, Rabelais, Shakespeare, and countless writers who preceded and succeeded these immortals.

In employing this device, a plot situation is woven into the script where two or more characters are discussing what they believe to be the same subject but which, in fact, concerns two completely different topics. In comedy, when this gimmick is written and performed perfectly, the laughter that greets its performance is long and loud, and like sex, even when it's done badly, it's still pretty good. And, coincidentally, almost all of the best juxtaposition routines are involved with sex.

One ancient example of juxtaposition, done in countless burlesque sketches, showed a newly married couple spending their nuptial night sharing a twin bed in the bride's parents' bedroom. To avoid embarrassing the honeymooners, a curtain was stretched between the bed they shared and the one the parents used. The four of them retired for the night, and the youngsters started to make love on one side of the curtain while the father, over the mother's whispered objections, tried to eavesdrop.

The groom, though ardent, was deterred by the cramped quarters, noisiness of their bed, and proximity of the parents. Finally, he whispered to his wife that they should take their suitcase, sneak out, and spend the night at a hotel. She agreed, the suitcase was placed on the bed, and they proceded to pack as quietly as possible. When they came to the high hat the groom wore at the wedding ceremony, the bride broke their silence by whispering in dismay, "It won't fit, it's too big."

The groom said, "I know, it's at least ten inches."

And on the other side of the curtain the father's eyes began to pop at what he heard.

Then the groom whispered to the bride, who was holding the suitcase, "Try to open it a little wider."

And she answered, "This is as wide as I can open it." Then she added, referring to the high hat, "Try to bend it or fold it."

The groom replied, "I know that some of them fold down to a smaller size, but mine doesn't."

And on the other side of the curtain, the astounded father keeps trying to peer over the curtain to see, as well as hear, their supposed sexual struggles. However, he is restrained from doing this by his wife.

The joke had several additional double-entendre lines and then came the big punch. This occurred when the couple tried to close the suitcase, but it was jammed with too many clothes and wouldn't shut all the way.

The bride said, "Maybe I ought to sit on it."

At this, Daddy, on the other side of the curtain, shook his head in amazement. The bride then sat on the suitcase but without success. It still wouldn't shut.

Finally the groom said, "Maybe it will help if we both sit on it."

Upon hearing this, the father pulled the curtain down, shouting, *"This* I gotta see."

That's an example of juxtaposition. A sophomoric example I'll admit, but it illustrates the point quite clearly. And the phrase, *"This* I gotta see," has become a cliché catch line with comedians and writers for countless years.

Like all writers, I've used this device, and what follows is an example from a script I wrote with Ray Singer for *Here's Lucy.*

The plot was simple. Lucy's boss and brother-in-law, Harry (Gale Gordon), had to have his tonsils removed. Harry was as apprehensive as a six-year-old kid, so Lucy acted as his surrogate mother and accompanied him to the hospital.

In the admittance office Harry was so nervous that the nurse said to him, "Go to the waiting room at the end of the corridor and relax there."

The action cuts to the waiting room where a brief conversation between a nurse and a man establish that this is "the Expectant Father's" room, and the man, named Phillips (actor Jack Collins), is expecting his fourth child.

THE NURSE EXITS. THERE IS A BEAT, AND
HARRY ENTERS. HE IS NERVOUS AND FIDGETY.

PHILLIPS

Hi.

HARRY

Hi.

PHILLIPS

Are you waiting too?

HARRY

Yes, I'm here for—

PHILLIPS

You don't have to tell me. I recognize the symptoms. I'm here for the same thing.

HARRY

You are?

PHILLIPS

Say, you look shaky. You'd better sit down.

PHILLIPS TAKES HARRY BY THE ARM AND LEADS HIM TO THE SOFA. BOTH SIT DOWN.

PHILLIPS
(continuing)

Is this your first time?

HARRY NODS "YES."

PHILLIPS
(continuing)

I've been through this three times.

HARRY
(reacting)

You mean this can happen . . . again?

PHILLIPS

It's been known to.

HARRY TENDERLY FEELS HIS THROAT AND TONSILS AND GULPS.

HARRY

Er, how big are they as a rule?

PHILLIPS

My first weighed seven pounds, three ounces.

HARRY
(reacts)

Didn't you have trouble finding collars to fit
you?

PHILLIPS TURNS SLOWLY AND GIVES HARRY A VERY PERPLEXED
LOOK.

HARRY

What did it look like?

PHILLIPS

It was the image of my wife.

HARRY'S EYES POP OPEN.

> HARRY
> (hesitantly)

Your wife must be a very unusual looking woman.

PHILLIPS REACTS SLIGHTLY, THEN CONTINUES TALKING.

> PHILLIPS

Ah, wait till you see yours. They don't look like much at first, but after a while they grow on you.

> HARRY

They do? . . . I guess that's why you had to come back three times.

> PHILLIPS

What a thrill you'll get when they first put the little thing in your arms.

> HARRY

They give it to you? . . . What are you supposed to do with it?

> PHILLIPS

You wrap it in a blanket and take it home. . . . What do you expect to do with yours?

HARRY

Well, I hadn't made any plans for it.

PHILLIPS

I'm going to send mine to college.

HARRY REACTS.

HARRY

I'd just as soon leave mine here.

PHILLIPS REACTS HORRIFIED AND LOOKS AT HARRY UNBELIEV-
INGLY.

PHILLIPS

What kind of man are you? Does your wife
know how you feel about this?

HARRY

What wife? I'm not married.

PHILLIPS STANDS UP AND STARES AT HARRY IN SHOCKED AMAZE-
MENT. THEN HE STARTS BACKING TOWARD THE DOOR.

PHILLIPS

Excuse me, I think I need some air.

AS PHILLIPS BACKS TOWARD THE DOOR, LUCY ENTERS, AND AS
PHILLIPS TURNS TO EXIT, HE BUMPS INTO HER.

PHILLIPS

Excuse me, lady.

PHILLIPS LOOKS BACK AT HARRY AND RAISES HIS EYEBROWS.

PHILLIPS

Tsk, tsk, tsk.

PHILLIPS EXITS. LUCY STARES AFTER HIM, PUZZLED, THEN TURNS TO HARRY.

LUCY

What's the matter with him? He acted awfully peculiar.

HARRY

You'd act peculiar too if you had a wife who looked like a tonsil.

LUCY FIGURES THE STRAIN IS BEGINNING TO TELL ON HARRY, SHOOTS HIM A LOOK, THEN SITS DOWN NEXT TO HIM.

The scene played very well. One of my peers said, "It was very funny, but contrived."

"Contrived" is a word we all hate, and a legendary incident took place when a producer dismissed a script with this denigrating word, and the writer snapped back, "Sure it's contrived. It took me three weeks to contrive it."

By their very nature all juxtaposition routines are contrived. Professional writers will continue to contrive such routines because they score high on the Richter scale of laughter, though critics may sneer and scoff at them.

Juxtaposition thrives best on double entendre, and one of burlesque's most famed skits is "The Baby Photographer."

In it a woman believes that because of a falling birth rate the government is sending men around to impregnate childless women. A man enters who the audience knows is a baby photographer, but she thinks he's a government baby maker.

The double entendres fly rapidly. The photographer asks her if she'd like to see samples of his work and shows her a folder containing eight large-size pictures of babies of every race and informs her, "I made all these in one afternoon." The amazed woman says, "You made eight in one day? That must be a record." The photographer said, "No, once I made thirty-two in an afternoon, but I got so overheated I had to take my tie off."

The woman says the babies look very nice. "But supposing I'm not satisfied with your work." He tells her, "If you're not happy with the finished product, return it, and I'll make you another one free. Don't worry, I'll keep coming till you're happy."

Convinced, the lady asks if they have to do it in any special place, and the photographer answers, "Any place at all. I've made them on kitchen tables, in bathtubs, on merry-go-rounds, and even seated on the toilet."

As the lady reacts, the photographer delivers the blackout line: "The one I'm proudest of I made under a tree in Central Park at high noon while thousands of people were watching *and the squirrels were gnawing at my equipment.*"

In the early days of TV the legendary *Burns and Allen* series used juxtaposition with great success. Through the years almost every program, if it stayed on the air long enough, tried it.

In the late seventies up through the 1983–84 season, *Three's Company* threaded this comedic misunderstanding through numerous plots with unfailing success. It's a great gimmick. Try it, you'll like it.

Hooking the Audience's Interest

Routines in comedy shows serve several purposes. They can further the plot, get laughs via situations, characters, or lines; and they can be priceless if they completely capture the audience's attention. If you can write something that intrigues the viewers, letting them know something funny is about to happen, but keeping them in suspense as to what, you will find them laughing throughout till you come to the final payoff.

Here are two examples. The first was done originally on Jack Benny's radio show and then repeated with equal success in TV. Jack and Mary Livingstone are attending an auction. Jack and Mary are engaging in a conversation while the auctioneer is simultaneously conducting his spiel and various participants are shouting out their bids for these items.

As the auction progresses the auctioneer proudly announces that the next item will be a much-sought-after historical trophy—an umbrella stand made from the leg of an elephant shot by the maharajah of some fictional principality in India.

Jack is amazed that anyone in Los Angeles would want an umbrella stand, especially such a grisly one made from the leg of a defunct pachyderm. He is even more amazed when a lady opens the bidding with an offer of $100, and when others begin raising her bid by increases of five and ten dollars, he whispers to Mary: "That's the most ridiculous thing I ever heard of. Offering so much money for a worthless piece of ugly junk." The bidding continues even higher, reaching over $150, and Jack keeps whispering to Mary about the stupidity of the people.

Mary "shushes" Jack and changes the subject. She whispers to him that she met Bob Hope the previous night and that Bob seemed upset because Benny hadn't sent him his check for appearing on Jack's program the week before. And during all this time there isn't a single attempt at a joke or a funny line, but the audience kept giggling. Just Jack and Mary whispering and the people at the auction increasing their offers by five dollars—or even two dollars. And as the bidding continues Jack says that he will naturally pay Hope for his appearance but he's not sure how much to send. Mary tells Jack that Hope should be paid his regular guest fee, and Jack asks, "What is Bob's regular guest fee?" Mary whispers, "Five thousand dollars?" A shocked Jack shouts, *"Five thousand dollars!"* And the auctioneer says, "Sold to the blue-eyed gentleman for five thousand dollars." The resulting scream lasted forty seconds.

Perhaps only a Jack Benny would have had the chutzpah to devote over two minutes of air time for a single laugh, but it paid off. Not only did he have faith in the routine, but he did not hire inexpensive actors to play the seemingly unimportant parts of bidders at the auction. Two of them were very expensive, Bea Benadaret, later to star in *Petticoat Junction,* was one, and famed vaudevillian Benny Rubin was another. And the auctioneer was portrayed by Hy Averback, well known as an actor who gained even greater fame as a director.

When the first draft of the script was finished, an executive raised the question as to the advisability of devoting so much time and money to a routine that had only one laugh in it, and with a live audience we couldn't be sure of the resulting laugh would be big enough to warrant it. Jack answered, "One thing I learned in all my years in show business is that if you've got the audience's interest, you've got the battle ninety percent won."

Jack was quoting a fact well known to all writers of drama and comedy. One of the standbys of literature is the mystery novel, and mysteries have always been popular on the stage and screen. Bob Hope was catapulted to stardom via his appearance in a series of comedy-mysteries, *The Cat and the Canary,* and *Ghost Breakers,* followed by his first picture with Bing Crosby, *Road to Singapore,* then alternating mysteries like *My Favorite Blonde* with more *Road* pictures.

Let's examine an excerpt from a *Here's Lucy* script that depended on hooking the audience's interest and holding it for a lengthy amount of air time before paying off. It was written in collaboration with Ray Singer, and our guest stars were Johnny Carson and Ed McMahon. The premise was based on the fact that Uncle Harry (Gale Gordon) was taking Lucy, her daughter Kim (Lucie Arnaz), and son (Desi Arnaz, Jr.) out for a big evening. A free broadcast at NBC. A panel discussion where four leading economists will discuss the origin of money. Naturally, Lucy and her children aren't too happy, and they are even less thrilled when they see that every one else in the NBC lobby is lining up to view the Johnny Carson show. Lucy tells them she has a plan to get in to the program. What follows is several pages, exactly as broadcast, except for cutting it down to just pertinent references to the routine.

INTERIOR.   LOBBY OF BROADCASTING STUDIO—NIGHT.

THIS IS THE SECTION OF THE TV STUDIO WHERE PEOPLE WAIT IN LINES TO BE ADMITTED TO TELEVISION BROADCASTS. THERE ARE THREE LINES OF PEOPLE GOING INTO ONE OF THESE STUDIOS. THE LINES ARE RATHER LONG, AND THERE IS A DOOR AND USHER AT THE END OF EACH LINE, AND THE USHERS ARE CHECKING EVERY-ONE'S TICKETS. THERE IS A LARGE BANNER OVER ALL THESE THREE DOORS READING "THE TONIGHT SHOW."

(LUCY HAS JUST INFORMED HER GROUP THAT SHE WILL GET THEM INTO CARSON'S SHOW.)

KIM

Without tickets? That's impossible.

LUCY

Maybe it isn't.

SHE DRAWS THE THREE OF THEM TOWARD HER AND SAYS CON-
SPIRATORIALLY:

You three get in line and take your cue from me.

LUCY GUIDES THEM TOWARD THE *FIRST* LINE GOING INTO THE
JOHNNY CARSON SHOW. THERE ARE THREE OR FOUR PEOPLE ON
THIS LINE AND ABOUT THE SAME ON THE OTHER LINES. KIM,
CRAIG, AND HARRY GET AT THE END OF THE FIRST LINE. LUCY
STEPS A BIT TO ONE SIDE AND WATCHES THE FIRST USHER AS HE
TAKES TICKETS FROM THE PEOPLE IN FRONT OF KIM, CRAIG, AND
HARRY. AS SOON AS KIM REACHES THE USHER, LUCY, A BIT TO ONE
SIDE, YELLS:

LUCY

Police! POLICE!

THE FIRST USHER RUSHES OVER TO HER.

1ST USHER (CARSON LINE)

Can I help you madame—what's the matter?

LUCY, WHO HAS OPENED HER PURSE, HOLDS IT UP.

LUCY

Someone stole my wallet out of my purse.

THE USHER INCLINES HIS HEAD TO LOOK INTO THE OPEN PURSE,
AND LUCY LIFTS IT UP, PRACTICALLY SHOVING IT IN HIS FACE.

WITH HER FREE HAND, SHE PUSHES UNCLE HARRY FORWARD
TOWARD THE ENTRANCE AND HARRY, KIM, AND CRAIG WALK IN.
(IF SHE IS POSITIONED SO SHE CAN'T PUSH HARRY, SHE MOTIONS
TO HARRY, KIM, AND CRAIG TO GO IN.)

LUCY

I know I had my wallet when I came in.

1ST USHER

There it is, ma'am—right under your handkerchief.

LUCY

LOOKS IN WALLET . . . FEIGNS SURPRISE.

Well, so it is. . . . You've been very helpful, young
man. . . .

HE GOES BACK TO TAKING TICKETS FROM A COUPLE OF PEOPLE
WHO JUST CAME IN. LUCY MAKES SURE HE IS NOT WATCHING
HER, AND SHE CROSSES TO THE *THIRD* LINE . . . AND GETS ON THIS
LINE. THERE ARE ABOUT TWO PEOPLE IN FRONT OF HER ON THIS
LINE, AND THEY PRESENT THEIR TICKETS TO THE USHER AND
ENTER. NOW LUCY REACHES THE THIRD USHER.

3RD USHER

Ticket, please.

LUCY

Oh, I don't want to see the show. My children

are in there, and I've got to give them an urgent
message.

3RD USHER

Lady, I've heard hundreds of excuses from
people trying to sneak in, but this is the daddy
of them all.

LUCY
(pleading)

I promise I'll be right out.

3RD USHER

That's what they all say.

LUCY
(pleading)

You've got to believe me.

REMOVING WRIST WATCH AS SHE SPEAKS.

Here, hold my wristwatch. If I don't come right out,
you can keep it.

3RD USHER

HE TAKES WATCH, LOOKS AT IT.

Well . . . all right. . . . You can go in.

LUCY

Thank you.

LUCY ENTERS AND DISAPPEARS FROM VIEW. THERE IS A FEW SE-
CONDS' BEAT DURING WHICH TIME SEVERAL LATECOMERS ENTER
THE LOBBY AND CROSS TO THE VARIOUS USHERS, PRESENT THEIR
TICKETS, AND GO INTO THE STUDIO. THE FIRST AND THIRD LINES
NOW HAVE PEOPLE ON THEM, BUT THE SECOND (MIDDLE) LINE
IS NOW EMPTY. LUCY NOW RE-ENTERS THE SCENE VIA THE MID-
DLE DOOR. SHE TALKS TO THE *SECOND* USHER.

LUCY

Excuse me, usher, I have to make an important phone call.

2ND USHER

POINTING TO A PHONE BOOTH IN CORNER.

There's a phone booth right over there.

LUCY

Thank you.

SHE TAKES ONE OR TWO STEPS TOWARD THE PHONE BOOTH AND
STOPS AS THOUGH SHE SUDDENLY REMEMBERS SOMETHING.

Oh, would you please give me a ticket so I can get back
in again.

2ND USHER

Certainly.

HE HANDS LUCY A TICKET.

LUCY

Thank you.

LUCY TAKES SEVERAL STEPS TOWARD THE TELEPHONE, AND THEN, MAKING SURE THE SECOND USHER ISN'T LOOKING, SHE TURNS AND CROSSES TO THE THIRD USHER (THE ONE WHO HAS HER WATCH).

LUCY

See, I came right out. May I have my watch back.

3RD USHER

Yes ma'am.

HE GIVES HER THE WATCH BACK.

LUCY

Thank you.

LUCY WALKS AWAY FROM THIS USHER AS THOUGH SHE'S GOING TO LEAVE THE STUDIO, THEN SHE CROSSES BACK TO THE 2ND USHER, HANDS HIM THE TICKET, AND WALKS INTO THE SHOW, AND WE

DISSOLVE TO:

Reread the routine. There is not one joke or attempt at a funny line. However, we got giggles and expectant chuckles throughout. The audience wondered what the payoff would be. Lucy's actions and going in and out of the various doors was practically choreographed. Toward the end they began to figure it out, especially when she got her watch back. She got a nice laugh with this and a big laugh and applause when she triumphantly entered the studio where Johnny Carson's show was being televised.

III
Standbys

Dirty Jokes

We have become increasingly permissive with the passage of time. Comics of either gender are currently amusing television viewers with material they would have hesitated using at stag affairs a decade ago.

Joan Rivers became a first magnitude star by telling jokes that might have closed down burlesque houses years ago. Yet she does them so well and with such obvious relish that the audience clamors for more. Example:

"Heidi Abramovitz. A tramp. Her legs have more time in the air than Lindbergh."

Lines that previously might have been banned in Boston and bleeped on television are now frequently finding their way into the media. True, these are cleaned-up versions, which the listeners can easily translate back to their lustier originals by substituting four-letter words for the politer euphemisms. And occasionally the original explicit Anglo-Saxon obscenity is used.

In April 1984, Richard Nixon made a couple of appearances on *60 Minutes*. During one interview Mr. Nixon said that when General Eisenhower couldn't make up his mind whether Nixon should continue as his running mate, he finally became impatient and told Ike, "Shit or get off the pot."

And when he was asked on *60 Minutes* what he thought of President John F. Kennedy, he quoted someone as describing Kennedy as "Stevenson with balls."

Several years ago comedian Orson Bean told the following anecdote on Johnny Carson's show: An anthropologist in Africa is trying to teach a native tribesman English. He took his pupil into the forest, pointed to various objects, slowly said their names, and had the native repeat them. He pointed to a tree, said, "Tree" and the native slowly repeated, "Tree." He pointed to a gorilla, said, "Gorilla," and the native repeated, "Gor-ill-a." He pointed to a lion and said, "Lion," and the native said, "Li-on."

This went on for some time till they came to a clearing where a couple was copulating. The embarrassed anthropologist didn't know how to describe love making so he simply pointed to the coupled couple and said, "Man riding a bicycle."

Instead of repeating the phrase, the native took his blow gun and killed the sexually involved man with a poisoned dart. The shocked anthropologist asked, "Why you kill him?" And the native answered, "Because him riding *my* bicycle."

The original version of this joke used the explicit four-letter word in lieu of "love making." Its deletion didn't detract from the audience's appreciative reaction. They howled long and loud, and I have a hunch that at least 90 percent of them mentally substituted the four-letter word for the phrase "love making."

Guests on the late night talk shows, and not exclusively comics or comediennes, seem to delight the audiences by relating the latest off-color laugh lines with slight variations from the verboten versions. And these are appearing with increasing frequency on most situation comedies. Today writers hearing a dirty joke try to think how it can be profitably laundered for public consumption. Handled properly, no sexual act or body function is too private for the public.

Another example of a bawdy boff being made acceptable for broadcasting: During the early days of our secret atomic plants, a man who worked at the top level priority in one of these nuclear hideaways was scheduled to go on a vacation to New York. In order to complete his work in time for his departure the following day, the man ate his lunch in the laboratory. He was so preoccupied with his chores that when he reached for his container of coffee, he unknowingly took a flask of the explosive heavy water used in making atomic bombs, and drank it.

As soon as he realized his mistake, he rushed to the doctor, who could find no immediate ill effects and suggested that while it was okay for him to go on vacation, he should report via phone every day.

That night the man flew to New York, and the following day he phoned the doctor and told him the heavy water seemed to have had an effect on him. He said, "Doctor, just a few minutes ago it made me do something I rarely do. I farted."

The doctor asked, "Where are you now?"

And the man answered, "I'm on the corner where Macy's used to be."

Funny, but strictly a stag story. That's what I thought until some months ago on a talk show I heard a comic tell this same yarn, except he substituted the word "belch" for fart. And the audience appreciated the anecdote and applauded as well as laughed at it.

Now this is an excellent switch, changing a laugh from naughty to nice. However, it also shows the changing attitudes of what is acceptable on the airways. Ten years ago "belched" would have been bleeped out, although he could have said "burped." And twenty years ago "burped" would have been "hiccupped."

Fart jokes keep popping up (pun not intended) on the more daring programs on the tube. On *Saturday Night Live* one female character wrinkled her nose in distaste and asked, "Who cut the cheese?"

All in the Family did several gags of this type but more subtly. Archie and Edith were in a hotel suite celebrating an anniversary. Edith was offstage when Archie opened a bottle of champagne with a loud pop. From the next room Edith's reproachful "Oh, Archie" got a large laugh.

Stag jokes can be bowdlerized by word substitution as shown when "belch" served for "fart." Other body or toilet functions can be referred to via such infant expressions as "making doo doo," "making tinkle," or "going potty." Instead of couples "screwing," they are "making love."

These instructions on cleaning up the dirties may be of only temporary value because with increasing laxity in censorship, television writers may soon find it more lucrative to start dirtying up the clean jokes.

Old Jokes

It's often been said that there are only seven basic jokes in existence. The only thing comedy writers do is switch them in any number of ways to fit plays, books, minstrels, radio, vaudeville, or video, to keep the public laughing.

In my capacity as producer and script consultant, I have often mentally wrestled with the problem of permitting an ancient laugh provoker sneaking into the script. If it were done cleverly, fitted the situation, and wasn't too hoary, I'd take a chance on it. After all, many people are too young to have heard it. Most of those who did hear it have probably forgotten it. And for those who heard it and remember it, if you switch it cleverly enough, they will laugh at it before they realize they have laughed at it in years gone by.

Sometimes jokes sound so legitimate that with the passage

of time they are told and retold in all sincerity by people who swear it happened. Example:

In the early 1940s we did a routine with Bob Hope, which went as follows: Someone said to Bob, "I understand you and Bing Crosby don't play golf together anymore."

"You're darn right," Bob answered indignantly. "Would you play golf with a man who cheats, lies, and refuses to pay off when he loses?"

"No," came the answer.

And Bob said, "Well, neither will Bing."

I now play golf, and at least once a year I hear someone tell this gag as though it happened with two members. It is always greeted with loud guffaws, and if the occasion ever presented itself where it could be worked into a script, I'd have no hesitation doing so.

Not only are old jokes reused but so are routines and ideas. Here's an example of the three-time usage of the same basic bit.

On a Jack Benny program I had Jack pick up a copy of *Playboy* magazine, open it to the centerfold, which got a laugh, and from behind it you heard Jack say wistfully, "Oh, if I were really only thirty-nine."

Second time on the *Here's Lucy* series, Gale Gordon also opened a copy of *Playboy* to the centerfold, again a laugh, and after a few seconds, from behind it you heard him sing, "To Dream the Impossible Dream."

Third time: Archie Bunker is in a hospital lobby waiting to be admitted for surgery. Edith's constant reassuring chatter bothers him so he suggests she read a magazine while he tries to nap. Edith picks up a copy of *Playgirl*, and its centerfold features completely nude men. Just showing the magazine, then the centerfold, got two laughs. Edith examined the centerfold from every angle, with varying facial expressions getting prolonged screams from the audience, which were compounded when Archie sleepily opened one eye, looked at what Edith was reading, and seconds later did the damnedest double-take.

One of the oldest laugh provokers in my memory was in an early all-talking picture. A man in a department store asked the floorwalker to show him to the sporting goods section. The floorwalker replied, "Yes, sir, walk this way."

The customer watched the clerk as he minced away and answered, "I can't walk that way unless I powder my thighs."

I guess that almost every comedy series on TV, if it survived long enough, did a version of this bit. I used it twice with excellent results. Once, in exactly the same situation, Jack Benny asked a floorwalker how to get to the men's clothing department. The answer was, "Walk this way," and the floorwalker glided away from Benny.

Jack observed him for a second then turned to the audience and said, "It's an old joke, but I'll do it."

In a 1983 episode of *Nine to Five* the boss had an injured leg in a cast and wanted the three girls to come into his office. "Walk this way," he ordered them, and the trio followed, each imitating his limp.

In Mel Brooks' picture, *History of the World*, a group of characters in togas were led by a man who limped. When he told the group "Walk this way," we were treated to a miniature limping parade. I doubtlessly missed this gag on many other shows, and hope to miss it in the future, unless someone gets a clever new twist on it.

In the recent hit movie, *My Favorite Year*, the biggest boff came from a famous old joke. Peter O'Toole portrayed a dipsomaniac movie star. In one scene a more than slightly soused O'Toole with a need to relieve himself, mistakenly enters a bathroom marked "Women." As we see him unzipping his fly, an actress (the late Selma Diamond) emerges from a stall, indicates the room and says, "Sir, this is for ladies only."

O'Toole, looking down at the unseen penis he is obviously holding in his hand, says, "Madam, so is this, but I have to run water through it occasionally."

I guess like old soldiers, old jokes never die. They don't even fade away. They are reincarnated in different films or programs.

Once, on a *Lucy* show, we had Sid Caesar playing a dual role. He played himself and an imposter who cashed phony checks using Sid's name. The imposter's big complaint was that, since Sid lost so much weight, he was forced to stay on a diet to look like him. Finally, the imposter is caught, and since he no longer can impersonate Sid, he goes on an eating binge.

I remembered seeing one of Sid's famed *Show of Shows* programs, where he played a man who starved himself to lose weight and then went off his diet with a vengeance, rushed into a delicatessen and screamed at the waiter, "Bring me a corned beef sandwich—*all fat.*" I asked Sid if I could use that line in our script. Sid laughed at the line and said, "Hey, that's a very funny joke."

I answered, "It should be, you used it about twenty-five years ago."

On another *Lucy* show the plot called for Lucy to get tickets to see Danny Kaye's TV show. Danny called the head of the CBS network, William Paley, telling him, "Mr. Paley, this is your favorite comic, Danny. . . . No, not Danny Thomas . . . Danny Kaye. *Kaye* . . . H. I. J. *K.* . . . No, not Danny *Hijk.*"

Danny loved the joke, not remembering he had used it on his radio show many years earlier.

There is an ancient anecdote that is always told as a true tale about a celebrity with a large nose. Over forty years ago I heard it about J. P. Morgan. A business associate invited him to dinner and cautioned his wife not to stare at the financier's prominent nose or act as if it were unusual. All went well till dinner was finished and the wife was about to serve tea, and she sweetly asked Morgan, "Do you take cream or lemon with your nose?"

This wound up as one of the biggest laughs on the *All in the Family* episode where Sammy Davis was going to drop by the Bunker house to pick up an attaché case he left in Archie's cab. Everyone was cautioned not to mention Sammy's lost eye or look to see if they could detect which was the artificial one. And of course Edith served tea and asked him, "Do you take cream or lemon with your eye?"

So don't be hesitant about using the golden oldies. I'm quite sure that most, if not all, of the jokes I've quoted in this chapter are new to 90 percent of the readers. But one word of caution. Never steal a widely quoted classic. You'll be roasted by the critics.

In the late 1960s a picture was released called *Waterhole No. 3. Time* magazine reviewed it saying, and this is not a verbatim quote, " 'Waterhole No. 3' is tasteless, trite and gory and has the temerity to use Jack Benny's famed 'Your Money or Your Life' line. We don't mind it being tasteless, trite and gory but we do object to them having the temerity to steal Jack's joke."

Remember, a joke is only old if everybody knows it—and nearly everybody knew "Your Money or Your Life."

Files

It was once widely thought that all successful comedy writers have vast and intricate filing systems, indexing and cross indexing almost every joke that was ever written. It was once true.

During the early days of radio when listeners were less surfeited and sophisticated than current TV viewers, files were used extensively, usually in conjunction with some original spicing added to the ancient material. A fabulous figure in those days was David Freedman, a talented man who had written several successful Broadway plays, many movie hits, books, and vaudeville acts. When commercial radio first blossomed, Freedman was in great demand. He supplied material for weekly radio programs, including Eddie Cantor's series that, if not number one, was close to it. Mr. Freedman lived in a penthouse that reputedly didn't need wallpaper because it literally had wall-to-wall files filled with jokes. This was where he ran his assembly-line comedy factory.

Freedman reputedly wrote outlines for the radio shows and had a staff of bright young wits who went through the files and extracted suitable jokes to flesh out the scripts. One who worked for him was novelist Herman Wouk. (Wouk followed this job with other writing assignments, including the coveted position of being on Fred Allen's staff.)

In his 1985 novel, *Inside Outside,* published in the spring of 1985, Wouk relates how his hero, a budding comedy writer, eventually turned lawyer, started his climb up the golden ladder working in a comedy file facility run by a man named Harry Goldhandler.

Wouk's job was, like his fictitious counterpart, to put file gags into the sketch scheduled for that week. If it were to be a legal skit, he and his coworkers would pull out all the jokes under the categories Lawyer, Judge, Court, Jury, Bail, Bailiff, Witness, Prosecutors, Defendants, Plaintiffs. The young writers would then assemble them in sequence, adding any original jokes they could think of, and turn them over to the boss.

Though there may be some writers today who refresh their memories with these files, probably using computers and other modern equipment, files have fallen in disfavor. The material is usually dated and accessible to every other writer. There would be nothing fresh and topical. And most important of all, the average competent comedy writer could quickly create more topical and funnier jokes on the subject before he could find useful ones in the files.

A case in point:

On *All in the Family,* Mort Lachman and I had to write a script from a story turned in by two freelance writers, Jim Tisdale and Calvin Kelly, who had gone elsewhere on to another commitment. The pivotal point of the story was Archie Bunker going to a hospital.

If Mort and I had used files we would have looked up such categories as Doctors, Nurses, Hospitals, Wards, Private Rooms, Medical Insurance, Blood Transfusions, Operations, Diseases, Illnesses, Visiting Hours, Visitors, Flowers, Candy, Gifts, Bedpans, Hot Water Bottles, Bad Food, High Fees, etc. We would have found such hoary jokes as, "He's feeling better, he just took a turn for the nurse," or, "Oh, I have a wonderful doctor, all he has to do is feel your pulse, and he can tell you exactly what you have—in your wallet."

We used no files; we followed the natural progression of a man being admitted to a hospital and the red tape questions invariably asked of a patient by an admittance nurse. Here are some excerpts from that routine.

NURSE

Where do you bank?

ARCHIE

At the Queens First Federal.

NURSE

Any reference?

ARCHIE

It's a pretty good bank.

NURSE

Do you own your own house?

ARCHIE

Yes.

NURSE

Is it encumbered?

ARCHIE

No, it's stucco and wood.

NURSE

Do you have medical insurance?

ARCHIE

Yes.

NURSE

What's the name of the company?

ARCHIE

Fiddle tie.

NURSE

Fiddle tie?

ARCHIE

Yes, Fiddle tie. Here's their insurance card.

NURSE
reading card

That's *Fidelity!*

None of these are file jokes. They each followed the normal progression of questions an admittance clerk would ask a prospective patient. And they were all tailored to fit Archie Bunker's character. Oh, yes, to add to the complications we added one more thing to aggravate Archie. We made the admittance nurse a member of a minority—a Puerto Rican, so well played by Liz Torres on this episode that she eventually became a semiregular on the series. Her questioning of the nervous Archie was interrupted by phone calls, during which she spoke Spanish as Bunker burned with impatience, leading to other opportunities for humor.

Today file material neither fits the characters nor the changing times. There is no file that can compete in wit and originality with the human mind.

Some top comedians today do have files but mainly of their own material. If they are doing a show and remember a big joke that fits the situation, they can consult their files and give the gag an appropriate switch. Also, there are certain subjects like inflation, the high cost of living, taxes, politics, traffic congestion, air pollution, and other topics that will always be with us, and files on them might serve the comedian well. For instance, during World War II there was gas rationing, and the fuel shortage became the target of many barbs. Then in the early 1970s we were all lining up at service stations, and I began to hear gasoline shortage jokes that were written over thirty years ago.

Many comedians like Bob Hope and Milton Berle have computer-type memories, which zing out a proper gag at the most suitable moment. Bob once had Berle appear in a cameo role on one of his specials. When the taping was over, Hope introduced his many guest stars to the applauding audience. The last one he presented was Berle, who ad-libbed, "How do you like that, folks. He had a big star like me come over for a thirty-second appearance and then he makes me wait half an hour to take a bow." The audience howled at this, and then Bob threw a line that broke them up again. This led to the two comics standing in front of an audience trading lines and keeping everyone in stitches for the better part of an hour.

Most of these were jokes each had used over their long illustrious careers.

After Berle and the rest of the cast left, we met with Bob to discuss cuts and changes. One of the writers said, "Gee, Bob, it was nice to see you standing there trading gags with Berle, who is supposed to be the fastest ad-libber in the business." Hope smiled and said, "Berle is definitely the fastest. He probably held back with me because we are good friends, it was my show and my audience. He has a mind like an IBM machine, throwing out the right joke instantaneously. Me, sometimes I've got to think for a half second."

Bob was being modest because I've seen him on occasion where he didn't need a split second to come up with the right answer years after he heard it. In 1956 I was with him in New York, and he was doing a guest appearance on Perry Como's program. For those of you who aren't aware of it, Como is probably the most relaxed man in the industry. The rehearsal had just finished, and the show would go on the air, live, in two hours. Hope and I started for Lindy's restaurant for a light bite. Suddenly Bob said, "Wait a few minutes. I just remembered something I want to tell Perry." He left me and seemed to return instantly, saying that the security man at Como's dressing room door was under strict orders not to admit *anybody*. "How about that," he said. "Como takes a one-hour nap before every program." I said, "Yes, and forty minutes during it." Bob laughed, and I forgot the incident until twenty-one years later Hope was a guest star on Merv Griffin's show, and Merv was telling Bob how laid back he was. Merv added, "Bob, you're probably the most relaxed man in show business." Without a fraction of a second's hesitation Hope began to relate the Como sleeping incident, which I myself didn't recall till he started it. Oh, yes, Bob gave me credit for the remark, which got me in trouble with my New York relatives, who thought this had just happened, and I had been in the Big Apple without even bothering to call them.

The Hope-Como story is to illustrate that files are used—but not card-indexed files. The ones you keep in your head, which are available instantly when the proper occasion calls for it. All writers have saved routines by remembering an oldie that exactly fit the situation.

There are many good indexed joke books on the market. Also weekly and monthly humor newsletters. By all means get them and read them. They can sharpen your memory and even throw you into a new version of an old laugh. But don't count on using file jokes. These are used mainly by nonprofessional humorists: doctors, lawyers, and businessmen who are called on occasionally to deliver speeches and wish to inject some humor. It may work well for them, but rarely for a successful professional comedy writer.

IV
SUBJECT MATTER

What topics are good subject matter for comedy? As the old song says, "Anything Goes."

Still, some subjects are more "natural" than others.

Sex

Sex is the fountainhead from which most comedic subjects spring. As the old joke goes, "Sex is very popular because it's so centrally located."

There probably is no series on the air today that doesn't find sex an almost guaranteed laugh subject. It can be used affectionately: Mike and Gloria Stivic are reminiscing about their first date. Mike: "Remember—I took you to a baseball game."

Gloria: "Yes, and you tried to score before the game started."

A putdown: Maude's husband Walter is getting dressed for a formal affair and can't find the studs for his shirt. Angrily he asks Maude, "Why is it you can never find a stud around here when you want one?" Her long look at him was the only answer this line needed to get a long loud laugh.

Another putdown: Mike and Gloria get into a heated argument in bed. Angrily Mike gets up, heads for the door and says, "That settles it, I'm going downstairs to sleep on the couch."

Gloria: "Go ahead for all the good you do me in bed."

You'll find senior citizen sex jokes every week on *The Golden Girls*—and almost every series starring anyone past middle-age. And on programs featuring preadolescents you'll hear double entendre lines spill innocently from the mouths of babes.

Golden Girls did an entire episode on whether widowed Betty White should go on an ocean cruise with a man. She was hesitant because she hadn't had sex since her husband died several years ago. Bea Arthur asked Rue McClanahan, "How long did you wait after your husband died to have sex?"

And Bea's mother (Estelle Getty) snapped, "Till the paramedics came."

The use of sex for story lines for scripts and subjects for routines is so widespread that at a recent affair Bob Hope said, "They are now showing men and women doing things on the screen that I wouldn't do in the privacy of my bedroom—even if I could."

Racial Humor

Racial humor has existed since the Neanderthals grunted gags about the inferiority of the Cro-Magnons or vice versa. From the moment there was a noticeable difference in groups of cavemen, one was the butt of the other's jibes.

Vaudeville starred different dialecticians who billed themselves as "German," "Irish," "Jewish," and "Italian" comedians. They covered every creed with scant regard for that race's feelings. Not all of their humor was derogatory, but much of it was. Vaudeville featured many black comics, but most of them were whites in burnt cork. One of the best known teams was Moran and Mack, who billed themselves as "Two Black Crows," and more than a few show business historians feel that the famed team of *Amos 'n Andy* was sired and inspired by Moran and Mack. On radio, *Amos 'n Andy* were portrayed by two Caucasians, Freeman Gosden and Charles Correll. When they went into television, they used black actors for the parts. Ironically, when the leads were done by whites on radio, the series enjoyed one of the longest, strongest careers in broadcast history. When it went on the tube starring black actors, it was boycotted by black groups, taken off the air, and supposedly filmed episodes are no longer in syndication.

During the days of radio, programs with various ethnic backgrounds enjoyed great popularity. Besides *Amos 'n Andy* there was *The Rise of the Goldbergs* (Jewish), *Life with Luigi* (Italian), *Baron Munchausen* (German), *The Life of Riley* (Irish) and others.

When radio metamorphosed into television, most of the ethnic rooted programs converted to the new medium. These were joined by a host of series covering every color and creed. Examples:

Sanford and Son and *Good Times* concentrated on black characters; *Chico and the Man* starred the late Freddie Prinz as a street-smart Chicano youngster; *I Remember Mama* gave us gentle Norwegian-accented humor; and Asians abounded on the tube with Sammee Tong playing the houseboy, Peter Tong on *Bachelor Father*. [Jack Soo was Detective Yemana on *Barney Miller*, Pat Morita played Matsuo Takahashi, who we knew better as Arnold on *Happy Days* and the star in *The Karate Kid* pictures.]

One of the longest running and most popular radio and TV series, *The Jack Benny Program*, probably featured more ethnic comic types than any other series. Early in radio he had Shlepperman, a Jewish accented actor followed by another Mr. Kitzel, in radio and TV. He also had Mel Blanc play the fiery tempered French violin teacher and also the monosyllabic Little Mexican of "Si, Cy, Sue" fame. And the Rochester-Benny combination was probably the longest and best loved integration on the air, and there was never any cry of racism.

Julia, which made its debut in 1968, was the first situation comedy that starred a non-Caucasian lady. Diahann Carroll played the title role, and Hal Kanter's pilot script made no reference to her race until well into the play, when she telephoned Dr. Chegley (Lloyd Nolan) and applied for a job as his nurse. Dr. Chegley immediately hired her sight unseen because she was so highly recommended to him by her former doctor boss. Cautiously Julia inquired, "Did he tell you I'm colored?" Chegley asked, "What color are you?" Julia replied, "I'm black." And Chegley asked, "Have you always been black or are you just trying to be fashionable?"

The only high rated series ever canceled because of protests was *Bridget Loves Bernie,* which was seemingly spawned by the hit play of sixty years ago, *Abie's Irish Rose.* The program's humor was based on the friction between Bridget's Catholic and Bernie's Jewish families. Complaints from both these religious groups brought a quick cancellation despite respectable ratings.

Racial humor will always be with us, and there is no reason to avoid it, but it must be handled tactfully and tastefully. Any blatant use of race as a basis for humor will result in an outcry sure to reach the ears of the networks and the sponsors.

Archie Bunker was able to get away with it (although *All in the Family* received large amounts of mail, pro and con, on Archie's attitude) because a rigid rule of the series was that no ethnic slur of his should go unanswered, usually by Mike and Gloria, and occasionally Edith.

On one program when he was severely scolded for some bigoted remark, he gave vent to an angry tirade that basically is a good rule to remember. He decried the fact that he couldn't poke fun at minorities and complained. "Geez, if you make a joke about the blacks, the NACPPP gets after you. If you say something about the Eyetalians, they take it up with the Pope, or go over his head to Frank Sinatra. And if you say something bad about the Jews, the whole Israeli Air Force will fly over and kicketh the crapola out of you." (As mentioned elsewhere, the line was originally, "If you tell a joke about Jews, you get hell from the Anti-Defecation League," but the censors blue-penciled it.)

Inebriation

The drunk is, and always has been, one of the most popular characters in literature. In drama he is usually a tragic figure. In comedy he is portrayed as a lovable buffoon always sure for a few boffs.

Charlie Chaplin did one of the most memorable movie routines about a drunk in his silent masterpiece, *City Lights*. It started when one night a millionaire (played by famed silent comedy star, Harry Myers) was returning home after having one or a dozen too many. He spots Charlie, forlorn and homeless on the street, invites him into his mansion, lavishes his largess on him, and makes him luxuriously comfortable.

"Came the Dawn," as the old cliché subtitle said, and the millionaire awakens cold sober, does not have the vaguest recollection of Charlie and has the Little Tramp thrown out. This is repeated in various ways with hilarious switches several times during the picture.

When the silent screen learned to talk, the drunk became an increasingly popular character because now the audiences could hear his slurred speech as well as see him stagger and stumble. Radio comedians were quick to copy, and the drunken orchestra leader, or musicians, became regulars on most programs.

Every decade or so the public laughed at a new lush. Hundreds of jokes were done about W. C. Fields' imbibing, many of the best pulled by the bulbous beaked comic at his own expense. One of them was when Fields was making a picture and went to his dressing room during a meal break and soon exited screaming, "Some varlet stole the cork out of my lunch."

Phil Harris and his supposedly boozing band were highlights on the *Jack Benny Show*. Once Phil told Jack he spent his vacation in the Alps hunting the famous brandy-carrying St. Bernards. Jack asked, "You hunted St. Bernards?"

And Phil answered, "Certainly, Jackson, they don't always find you, you know."

Bob Hope had no running role of a souse on his show, but he had his routines interrupted many times when drunks would wander in. Bob squelched one once by saying, "Buddy, that breath of yours would start the windmills on an old Dutch painting." That joke still pops up on the tube pretty regularly.

Dean Martin's drunkenness became almost as well known as Benny's thriftiness. Martin took advantage of the situation by doing gags about himself: "I had an accident last night. I was coming home from a party when somebody stepped on my hand."

Getting loaded has served as the story line for episodes on many shows, but invariably they follow one basic rule. The person, especially if he or she is a regular on the series, must be imbibing the alcohol innocently and unknowingly. The viewers will accept this, and they also will accept the fact that someone has to drink the liquor for survival.

Once Lucille Ball was selected to extol the virtues of a health tonic on a television program, and as she plugged it, she was supposed to taste it to show how palatable it was. "Vitameatavegavin" was its name, and alcohol was its main, and seemingly only, ingredient. Each time Lucy said the name "Vitameatavegavin," she was to take a sip of this soothing syrup. Now "Vitameatavegavin" is hard to handle sober, and each time she tripped over some syllable, she had to start fresh and once again tipple a taste of the concoction. There are certain scenes that the written word cannot adequately describe with full honors. This is one of them. I've watched it numerous times, and it is an exemplary illustration of how writing the right material for the right performer can create a comedy classic.

Red Skelton's "Guzzler's Gin" routine has been one of his standbys for years.

The drunk is almost always good for laughs, but a word of warning. One of the most prestigious organizations in the industry, The Caucus, composed of producers, writers, and directors, sent a December 1985 memo to the members of the guilds governing these occupations. They listed several suggestions on restricting the depicting of drinking in the media. Briefly, they urge, "Try not to glamorize drinking as sophisticated ... don't associate drinking with macho pursuits ... don't show excessive drinking without consequences."

Because of these, and similar admonitions, all writers realize it's unfeasible to involve a character in a position where his condition would endanger innocents. I don't think any program today would consider using a gag done on the air several times over past seasons that went as follows: The scene, a party as it's breaking up. A very intoxicated guest starts to leave and futilely searches his pockets complaining, "I can't seem to find my car keysh." The concerned host asks, "You're not going to drive home like that?" And the drunk answers, "Shertainly, I'm in no condishun to walk."

Physical Frailties

By nature human beings are cruel. It's been said that if you slip on a banana peel, it's a painful experience; if your neighbor takes the same fall, it's hilarious. Physical differences are funny and possibly the most joked about is obesity.

An early movie comedian whose career was cut short by a scandal was Roscoe Arbuckle, but who knew his given name was Roscoe? He was famed as Fatty Arbuckle, and theater marquees and newspaper headlines identified him as "Fatty." In vaudeville comics built their acts around their excess weight. In radio, Don Wilson, long-time announcer for Jack Benny, was the constant butt, and I do mean butt, for everyone's jibes. One of many took place on the opening program of a new season when Wilson greeted Benny by saying, "Well, Jack, it looks like we're both carrying a little extra weight since the summer." Jack answered, "Look behind you, Don, I'm carrying mine, you're dragging yours."

A man's height, or lack of it, is fair game. Wilt Chamberlain and Herve Villechaize, despite their difference in stature, have been equal targets for humor. Mickey Rooney always derides his lack of height in interviews. He is reported to have said, "I could have been tall but my agent turned it down." *The Golden Girls* devoted an entire episode to the fact that Betty White was dating a midget. Humor stemmed from the fact that, when she brought him to the house to meet her friends, they discussed in advance that they would avoid all references to his height. But when he arrived, everything they said was an inadvertent reference to it. For instance, when she served hors d'oeuvres, Rue McClanahan asked him if he wanted one —a shrimp. It seems corny and cliché in print, but the way they handled it provided pure comedy. And the blackout of the episode offered a reverse racial twist, when the midget told Betty he couldn't marry her because his parents would object since she wasn't Jewish.

Baldness and toupees will always be with us. A current scapegoat is Howard Cosell who gets ribbed about his "rug." Once on the Jack Benny show we scored a daily double on infirmity when Jack came home and asked Rochester, "Were there any calls for me?" Rochester: "Yes, your dentist and your barber called." Jack: "Did they leave any messages?" Rochester: "Yes, they both said you can pick them up tomorrow."

Noses are not neglected. Jimmy Durante made his the foundation of his career. Danny Thomas' giant economy size had him say, "If you're gonna have a nose, have one. Don't have one of those little warts. Have something you can breathe through, which is what it was intended for." Bob Hope's ski-sloped schnozz has become a trademark in all caricatures and cartoons. Though he has tapered off, Bob will still pull lines like the time he was doing a mystery sketch with a guest star and the guest said, "We'll get to the bottom of this by hook or crook." And Hope answered, "I'll thank you to leave my nose and my brother out of this."

Bad eyesight. On the surface this looks like the least likely subject to succeed, but one of the longest running animated cartoon characters is Mr. Magoo. Near-sightedness is a subject for comedy, not pity. Silent screen star Ben Turpin had one outstanding comedic asset: crossed eyes. Sammy Davis, Jr., laughs at his loss of an eye. A regular character on *All in the Family*, and its successor, *Archie Bunker's Place*, was Mr. Van Ranseleer (Bill Quinn), a blind habitué of the bar. Every episode, Archie would wave his hand in front of Van Ransaleer's face as though to assure himself he was sightless.

One laugh we got from his character was the time the others in the bar found that he had been visited by a prostitute, and they all expressed surprise.

Van Ransaleer said, "Why shouldn't I have a lady friend? I'm blind, not dead."

Another sequence we had was in the bar where Archie, now the owner, was screaming because something was misplaced. Van Ransaleer observed that for a blind man everything must always be in exactly the same spot so he will know. He then said, "Once I had a cleaning woman who mixed up the contents of my medicine cabinet. I reached for my Preparation H but got my Dentu-Grip instead."

Archie asked, "What happened?"

And the reply was "Nothing for six days."

The routine never broadcast, because the censor thought it a bit too racy for the air.

The female figure has been consistently supplying comedy material. There have been jokes about feminine endowments, front and rear, ever since I can remember. Comedians found that breasts could get laughs, and with the advent of Mae West's popularity they became acceptable.

Jack Benny once got a double laugh by saying, "As I was walking down Wilshire yesterday, I saw Jane Russell walking toward me. As she got nearer, I realized it was Fred Allen. Gee, those bags under his eyes are terrible."

The reverse is true, too. Joan Rivers' figure, or lack of it, is almost always included in her monologues. I remember the first joke I heard about skinny girls back when I was a kid. Some vaudeville comedian said, "I knew a girl so thin that once she swallowed an olive, and four fellows left town." When that joke was deemed too blue for certain theaters, it was switched by saying the girl was so thin that, if she drank grape juice, she could be used as a thermometer.

Kidding about physical handicaps, if they are not horrendous, can be funny. Yes, they're cruel, but if you analyze it, most humor is cruel. It's your obligation to write the ones that make audiences laugh, not groan.

What follows is an abbreviated index of other subjects which are among the many that lend themselves to humor.

Other Reliables

Holidays

They have always been a special event for scripts, initiated during the radio days and transferring to the tube as a natural subject. Thanksgiving shows were based on shopping for the feast and usually a routine about how hoggish the musicians were. Bob Hope, about eating with the boys in the band, "I bent my head to say grace. By the time I looked up, they were finishing dessert . . . I spilled some gravy on my shoe, and before I could wipe it off the pianist ate it . . . You should see how fast the drummer ate. It was the first time I ever saw anybody get sparks out of a knife and fork."

Jokes about Christmas shopping and how crowded the stores were began many weeks before Yuletide. Jack Benny did an annual Christmas shopping show with sequences showing the various cast members making their purchases. The programs always concluded with Jack driving Mel Blanc, playing a clerk, into violent hysterics because he kept coming back to exchange some insignificant gift again and again and again.

The obvious drawback in doing shows about these holidays is that, when the series is rerun, the cast is doing jokes about it being a "White Christmas," while the viewers may be turning up their air conditioners in the hottest summer they remember.

The Bible

This is normally a kid-glove subject. Gentle jokes have been made about biblical sayings, usually innocently misquoted by children. Or a man telling an unattractive woman: "If God had taken a good look at you, there would have been an eleventh commandment." As a rule, writers steer clear of the Holy Book. Except on *All in the Family.* The theological arguments between Mike and Archie were many and memorable. Archie Bunker, by his own admission, was the acknowledged authority on the Bible and expounded many interpretations of it.

He insisted that his grandson be baptized and eventually, without Mike and Gloria's consent or knowledge, he practically kidnapped the infant and then, when the minister refused to accommodate him, he baptized the boy himself in a touching yet hilarious sequence. Archie vowed that he'd make little Joey a good Christian if he had to break every one of the Ten Commandments to do it.

He told Mike that the child had to be baptized, because people who weren't couldn't gain admittance to Heaven. Mike asked if this meant that no Jew would be allowed up there. Magnanimously, Archie gave solace to followers of that faith by stating that they could get in because all Jews were baptized. A startled Mike asked how and when, and Archie said, "When Moses crossed the parted Red Sea, he got his feet wet so all Jews was baptized."

There were numerous head-to-head screaming debates about the existence of heaven, and once Edith sided with Archie and said there was a heaven. When Mike asked her to describe it she said, "Heaven is quiet and peaceful and everybody loves everybody else. It's like *The Dinah Shore Show.*"

The arguments weren't always about Heaven. They took the opposite direction and debated the existence of Hell. Mike derided Archie's belief in hell, and once their dialogue went as follows:

ARCHIE

Let me ask you—have you ever told anyone to go to hell?

MIKE

Well—yes, but—

ARCHIE

Well where did you want them to go—to Disneyland?

MIKE

Arch, that's just an expression.

ARCHIE

Ohhhhhhhh—just an expression. Well, wait till you get down there, and the devil and all his nimps are running around with their hot pitchforks waiting to stick them into your heinie. . . . I want to be there when you look the devil in the eye and say, "I ain't burnin' down here. That's just an expression." Boy, the devil is gonna give you the hee-haw.

MIKE

Archie, you say that Hell is down in the bowels of the earth?

ARCHIE

Right down in the bowels of the earth where nobody living can find it.

MIKE

I don't know—Exxon is drilling all over the place, they're bound to find it.

Because of the nature of the show, *AITF* was able to tackle topics that most other programs avoided. And unless you are writing something so good that the resulting laughs will outweigh the complaints your script will incite, it's best to exclude religion and the Bible from comedy.

Prostitution

When I first started writing this book, the subject of whores was something that was hinted at in veiled double entendre

jibes. While dramatic shows used whores and harlots frequently, it was a no-no for comedy unless well disguised. Then
on their show of October 4, 1986, *The Golden Girls'* entire plot
premise was prostitution. Bea Arthur, Betty White, and Rue
McClanahan happened to be in a hotel where rooms are
rented by the hour rather than the night, and they wound up
in the slammer with a bunch of tarnished ladies of the evening. Estelle Getty (Sophia) came to bail them out, and she
was incensed that the police were stupid enough to mistake
the three Golden Girls as hookers. In effect she told the trio,
"How could the police be dumb enough to think that men
would spend money to sleep with you." The resultant laugh
was long and loud, there was no shocked "oooohhhs," so I
guess in the proper place red lights are no longer blue-penciled.

Politics

Another winner. But you must be prepared for the consequences. The same joke told by the same comedian about the
same politician on the same program will invariably bring
mail. There will be those who claim the joke pro-Republican.
Others who say it is pro-Democrat.

Are there any repercussions in poking fun at the Presidents?
Not in my experience. The shows I have been with have told
jokes about every President from Roosevelt to Reagan with
never a comment from any of them. Except once. When Ger-
ald Ford was heading the country, his wife, Betty, once was
headlined in every newspaper when she said, in effect, that she
wouldn't be surprised if her son used marijuana and her
daughter had an affair. This outraged Archie Bunker, that
self-appointed guardian of public morals, and he began berat-
ing Mrs. Ford. Mike defended her, and said she had every
right to free speech. Archie concluded the lengthy harangue
by stating, "It's not the First Lady's place to go around saying
stupid things. That's the President's job."

The audience responded to the routine with a huge laugh

and applause greeting the final line. A few days later we heard that the White House requested a cassette of this show. It was sent with trepidation and expectation of some sort of official reprimand. And some time later we heard that the White House thought it was very funny.

Politicians and presidents have always been fair game for humorists whether they were cartoonists, commentators, or comedians. One of the first jokes I remember happened in the early thirties when Babe Ruth was signed for the then-unheard-of astronomical salary of $80,000 for the season. Newspapers wrote editorials, wondering why a baseball player should earn more than President Herbert Hoover, whose annual income was only $75,000. Will Rogers wrote in his daily column, "I think that the president will get as much money as Ruth when you hear a hundred thousand fans screaming for Hoover to knock one over the fence." When the great Bambino was asked if he deserved more money than the president, he answered, "Certainly, I had a better year than the President."

During the days of radio and live television, the week before election day saw every comedian doing routines on the coming event. In California the ballots are filled with various propositions, and one of Bob Hope's gags was "Election Day is the only day that a lady can say 'Yes' to a proposition and still be a lady." In 1948 Harry S Truman upset Tom Dewey, and every political pollster. Jack Benny discarded an entire sequence so that the writers could prepare a sketch ridiculing the Roper and other famous polls, which predicted an easy Dewey victory.

In more recent years almost all shows had laughs at the expense of President Carter's beer-drinking brother Billy, or President Ford's inability to chew gum and walk at the same time. A running gag with Chevy Chase on the early *Saturday Night Live* shows was his imitation of Ford falling down, and during a symposium on humor in the late summer of 1986 President Ford did a skit in which he tripped Chase to make him fall. Reagan's age is a frequent funny topic, and I can't recall how many times I've heard the line about Ronnie's hair being prematurely orange.

All of our statesmen have learned the more you're in the public eye the more highly visible target you make, and because of that they rarely voice objections. Possibly the only show that was ever cancelled because of political and controversial material was *The Smothers Brothers* on CBS. But times have changed since then—the jokes that got them cancelled might be considered mild now.

Round Pegs in Square Holes

This is usually where you have one sex discussing the other's domain. Most frequently used is the females' alleged ignorance of sports, and the dialogue usually goes like this:

Husband: "Wow what a game. The Lakers beat the Celtics in overtime."

Wife: "Gee, how many innings did they play?"

And programs still get laughs from men doing, and botching, household chores.

Age

The advancing age of a person has always been an easy but surefire laugh provoker. Jack Benny remained thirty-nine for more years than most fans can remember. Once someone asked, "Jack, did you see Halley's Comet?" And Phil Harris snapped, "Twice."

I believe it was on Carson's show where someone said that Reagan could recite Lincoln's Gettysburg Address. The answer was, "Ronnie ought to remember, he was there when Lincoln first said it."

Homosexuals

For years male homosexuals were frequently portrayed on the airwaves via simpering stereotypes. A lisp and a limp wrist was all the character needed to get a guaranteed quota of laughs. They appeared mainly in variety show sketches and occasionally a single shot on a sitcom.

Possibly the best remembered comedy shows on the subject started as a one episode assignment on *All in the Family.* Archie occasionally earned extra money driving a cab nights. Once he came home very excited. He was a hero. A woman passed out in his cab. He stopped, pulled over to the side, gave her mouth-to-mouth resuscitation, and when an ambulance arrived, they told him he probably saved her life. As she was taken to the hospital, he put a piece of paper with his address on it in her hand in case she wanted to show her gratitude.

The next scene opened with Archie offstage upstairs. The doorbell rang. Edith opened the door and admitted a rather attractive generously built lady who wanted to thank and re-imburse her rescuer. Further dialogue revealed that she passed out because she was rushing from one theatrical en-gagement to another. She further informed Edith that her name was Beverly LaSalle, and she was a female impersona-tor, to which Edith replied, "If you're a woman, that's the best thing to be." Then Beverly revealed that she was really a he acting as a she. When Archie learned that he "mouth to mouthed" a man, he vigorously rubbed the memory of it off his lips. Beverly and Edith became good friends.

In the second show Beverly surprised Edith some weeks later by coming to the Bunker house in Queens. Beverly in-formed her that after just three weeks she had been booked again to star in the local nightclub. When Edith asked, "Isn't that very quick?" Beverly smiled and said, "Yes, but for some reason they love me here in Queens." In this story Archie wanted to get even with a man who always played practical jokes on him—so he arranged a blind date for the man with Beverly enticing his friend with the cliché line, "Have I got a girl for you."

We then prepared a third script which turned into a two-parter. Edith invited Beverly to Christmas dinner, and Beverly arrived in time for the tree trimming. They discovered they needed some more ornaments, so Mike and Beverly, now attired as a man, walked to the store to get them. We later learn that a gang of hoodlums jumped the pair and beat them up. They concentrated on Beverly because Beverly was "different." Beverly died.

The second installment centered around Edith refusing, for the first time anyone could remember, to go to church. Edith had lost her faith in a God who would permit such a thing to happen. Archie, who was genuinely upset by Beverly's death, was even more upset at his wife's atheistic sentiments. He never went to church himself, but Edith never missed a Sunday till now. He wanted Edith to go because he said, "When you come home after listening to one of the minister's sermons, you have a peaceful look on your face like you was chloroformed." Eventually Edith made her peace with God, but the writers and producers never made peace with themselves for killing off a character too quickly. We could have gotten several additional episodes out of Beverly LaSalle because, as Archie once complimented her, "You know, Beverly, for a gal, you're quite a guy."

I believe *All in the Family* was the first comedy series to tackle the touchy topic of lesbians. The episode was called "Cousin Liz" and won the 1978 Emmy as best comedy script. (Written by Bob Weiskopf and Bob Schiller, story by Barry Harmon and Harve Broston.) A running theme in the series was that Edith had elderly uncles, aunts, and cousins galore who were either sick or dying, and Archie would never go to see them when alive or attend their funerals when deceased. Once Edith begged him to join her in visiting a terminally ill aunt, pointing out that the woman was at death's door. Archie yelled, "Edith, she's been at death's door for over thirty years and never made an honest effort to crawl through."

The "Cousin Liz" program started off with Edith telling Archie that her Cousin Liz had died. For the first time, Archie is genuinely upset by the death of one of Edith's relatives because Liz was a contemporary of theirs. In fact, Archie dated her several times and had a teenage crush on her. He agreed to go to the funeral because Liz was the only one of Edith's relatives he liked: "She was the one good egg in a barrel of rotten apples."

The revelation of Liz' sexual preference came after the unseen funeral, in the house of Cousin Liz' roommate, Veronica. Till this moment it is doubtful that any viewer suspected that the deceased Cousin Liz and Veronica were anything but two schoolteachers sharing an apartment to split expenses. The audience knew that Cousin Liz was feminine and attractive, and as a youth Archie had kissed her several times on dates. The actress portraying Veronica was beautiful—and beautifully played by K. Callan. (She uses the initial "K." as her name.)

In a very touching scene Veronica talks privately with Edith in her bedroom. The bedroom she shared with Cousin Liz. The bedroom with only one double bed in it. She wants to keep a tea set that was an heirloom in Edith's family for over a century. Edith is sympathetic, but says the tea set belongs in the family. Veronica tells her that she and Liz were very close, something like family. No, not like sisters, closer. Then it dawns on Edith who says the one word "Oh" several times with different inflections all getting laughs. She comforts Veronica, saying that it must be awful to love someone and have to keep it a secret.

Archie enters the bedroom to inform Veronica that some postfuneral guests were leaving, so she exits. Archie dances a joyful jig as he tells Edith that one of the guests knew about antiques and the tea set was solid silver and worth over $2,000. Edith then informs the astounded Archie of the relationship between the girls. After several suitable facial takes, Archie says, "You mean—Liz was a Lez?" When the answer is in the affirmative, Archie quickly uses the back of his hand to wipe away Cousin Liz' kiss of forty years ago. (A repeat of the gesture he used years earlier when he learned he gave mouth-to-mouth to a man.) Edith exits to the living room where all the guests have left, and Veronica is alone. She tells Veronica she can keep the tea set and Archie turns to Veronica and yells, "I only got one thing to say to you people—why don't youse turn yourselves around." As the Bunkers prepare to leave, Veronica impulsively hugs and kisses Archie, and when she finishes, he says, "There! Didn't that do something for you."

That was over ten years ago, and with the new freedoms and standards today, homosexuals are seen more and more frequently and not always as the object of jokes. There is a successful cable comedy called *The Brothers.* The series concerns three brothers, two of them straight and one not.

Ignorance

If you have a character who thinks he knows far more than he actually does, you'll get frequent laughs by taking advantage of it.

Archie Bunker was wonderful with this, and here are a pair of examples:

"Remember, I was in WW2. The big one. The war that made the world safe from democracy."

Another time Mike admitted he made a mistake and told Archie he was sorry. Archie bellowed, "Being sorry doesn't help. Mrs. O'Leary's cow was sorry but Cincinnati burned down anyway."

Jack Benny got a lot of mileage out of ignorance via his penchant for being an expert on everything, especially sports. We usually used this device with a prominent guest star in the field. The audience always knew in advance the importance of the guest. Example:

On radio we did a scene in the dining car of the Superchief and opened it with a waiter seating a man at a table saying, "And good luck in the big game, Mr. Leahy." All listeners knew it was the big football game between the Leahy-coached Notre Dame team and USC.

Moments later Jack was seated at the same table, struck up a conversation, and asked if his dining companion was going to see the football game. When the answer was yes, Jack immediately launched into reasons why USC would whip the poorly coached Notre Dame eleven.

We used the same device with Leo Durocher among others, and on one of Jack's early TV shows he began to correct Ben Hogan's swing, causing the greatest golfer of his time to get twisted like a pretzel before Jack was satisfied he was doing it right. Of course, Jack didn't know he was giving instructions to Ben Hogan, but even when Jack knew the celebrity, he'd still brag. He put his foot in it when future Supreme Court Justice Earl Warren was governor of California and a guest on the show. Jack tried to impress the governor with all the facts he knew about Califorina, and boasted that he got his information from a man very high in politics, Edward Flynn.

Impressed, Warren asked, "Do you mean Edward J. Flynn?"

Smugly Jack said, "Yes, do you know him?"

And Warren answered, "I should, he's my chauffeur."

Nonsequiturs and Illogical Logic

Gracie Allen was the queen of this type of humor. Here are some Gracie-isms. One day Gracie was busy in the kitchen boiling water, putting it in jars, and then storing the jars of hot water in the freezer. When her neighbor Blanche asked her why she was doing this, Gracie explained, "In case I ever want hot water in a hurry, I thaw out one of these bottles."

Gracie's explanation of why she put salt in the pepper shaker and pepper in the salt shaker was because people were always getting the two of them mixed up, and now when they get them mixed up they'll be right.

She once told George Burns that her brother was a pickpocket. When Burns reminded Gracie that her brother had only one finger on his hand, Gracie answered, "I know, that's why he only steals doughnuts."

Gracie once told Blanche, "I heard some terrible gossip

about you from a woman." When Blanche wanted to know what it was, Gracie said, "I don't know. I forgot it the minute I told it to her."

A conversation between Blanche and Gracie:

Blanche: I just got a phone call from Lucille Vanderlip, and she told me Marie Bates got a beautiful diamond ring from her husband.

Gracie: I can't believe it.

Blanche: Why not?

Gracie: If Lucille's husband gave another woman a diamond ring, she'd be the last one to mention it.

And once when Burns and Allen were supposed to make a guest appearance on Jack Benny's program and Gracie didn't show up, George started to explain, "I told Gracie I'd like some Philadelphia cream cheese." And both Jack and George finished the sentence simultaneously saying, "So she went to Philadelphia to get it."

Controversial Topics

Prior to 1971 writers steered clear of anything that smacked of controversy. Then came *All in the Family.* They did episodes on rape, attempted rape, infidelity, impotence, vasectomy, mastectomy, miscarriages, lesbians, transvestites, and other subjects that were deemed unfit for comedy.

Then producers learned that a comedy can do a public service by handling these touchy topics tastefully and mixing them judiciously with laughs. The viewers accepted them, and they had far higher ratings than documentaries that seemed too heavy and preachy. Not only that, but these programs were excellent for exploitation and reaped rewarding ratings. They pop up with a great frequency these days. Child molestation has been a topic on several comedies including *Family Ties.* Drugs have been handled by *The Bill Cosby Show,* and Archie Bunker was hooked on uppers and downers for a few episodes. Recently, *Mr. Belvedere* was given special commendation for a program discussing AIDS from a young boy's viewpoint.

The list of sitcoms that aired previously unmentionable matters is long and impressive. One word of caution: If you get a producer's okay to do an episode of this type, be armed with the name of a reputable organization that does public service work in this field and have the assurance that they will cooperate with you.

Taboos

Urination is doubtlessly a tasteless topic, yet it has been done on many programs with hilarious results. Estelle Getty on *Golden Girls* said she urinates every morning precisely at seven—the only trouble is that she doesn't get up till eight. On a *Maude* episode her husband Walter (Bill Macy) gave a lesson in the fine art of masculine urination to grandson Philip where he said that a gentleman always does it against the side of the bowl so he won't make a loud splash. . . .

In the previously cited examples urination was talked about or implied, but viewers did not actually see any urine, genuine or simulated, and there were no repercussions. However, when *Saturday Night Live* premiered its new season in November 1985, the series was soundly scolded for opening with a scene based on the then current furor over whether baseball players would have to submit to urinalysis to detect drugs. They showed a tray holding several small containers filled with what was supposedly urine, and a network executive announced that NBC was going to give urine tests to its stars for the same reason they were given to athletes. The executive discussing this was not an actor but the network's head of programming, Brandon Tartikoff, a man of sound judgment and good taste who evidently let his desire to help *SNL*'s sagging ratings cause him to participate in this little charade.

(During a January 7, 1986, talk to out-of-town TV critics at the Century Plaza Hotel in Los Angeles, Brandon Tartikoff admitted he probably erred appearing in the season opening *Saturday Night Live* spoof on urine tests. He said, "I realized from your reactions that there was probably some error in that judgment. The routine will be deleted from reruns.")

Jokes about genitalia are verboten, but one occasionally slips by on late talk shows in a veiled reference to the size of a man's organ—or lack of it. The only time I heard a joke of this nature on a network comedy came on CBS during the 1985 December debut of their new series, *Foley Square*, in which Margaret Colin played a lady assistant district attorney. She had taken a personal ad in a magazine in an effort to meet men. The final scene of the episode showed her reading some of the less savory replies. She picked one up, scanned its contents with distaste and phoned the sender and said to him, "Women don't appreciate men who send naked pictures of themselves in the mail. It's a Federal offense, although in your case a minor one."

The only other occasion I remember a prime-time reference to the insufficiency of the male organ was during the famous Academy Awards broadcast when a naked man streaked across the stage. There was an uproar from the surprised audience at this unscheduled flasher, and David Niven, who was at the microphone at the moment, gazed after the disappearing nudist and observed, "It's amazing what lengths some people will go to show their shortcomings."

Doing jokes about celebrities of advanced age is dangerous because they can depart before the show arrives. Sometimes the person is still alive when the program is originally aired, but, oh, those reruns. I once wrote an Emmy nominated script (with Ray Singer) where Lucy tried to get Jack Benny's account for the bank for which she worked. She tells Jack, at his home, that if she lands his account, the bank will give her a bonus, and she'll use the extra money to pay for violin lessons for her nephew. "Who knows," she said flatteringly, "he may be a second Jack Benny." Jack said,

"The world doesn't need a second Jack Benny—the first one ain't gonna go." When this was filmed in front of a studio audience, it got a good laugh.

When I saw the episode rerun years later, just a few weeks after Jack had passed away, I didn't think it was funny.

At the opening of this chapter, it was noted that as far as subject matter is concerned, anything goes. Let your good taste be your guide.

Death

Of all the taboo subjects, death is the hardest to write about. One learns early in life that death is tragic; death is final; death is sad and sorrowful. Death is nothing to laugh at.

Wrong.

Handled properly it has always been and will be one of comedy's most hilarious subjects. True, there are rules that must be followed. The deceased must be a character not liked by the audience or completely unknown to them. The demise of a well-liked character has to be handled quite seriously.

When, in the middle seventies, it was announced on *M*A*S*H* that Lt. Col. Henry Blake (McLean Stevenson) was killed in a crash, it was done quickly and soberly and then dropped. Fans were furious, but Stevenson wanted to leave the series, and the accident was a realistic way to explain his absence.

On the Jack Benny show we had Mary Livingston talk about her sister's new boyfriend—an undertaker. "He's the most progressive undertaker in town. He has a convertible hearse. His slogan is 'Get a little brown, before we lower you down.'" We repeated it several times on radio and TV, always getting laughs on both "convertible hearse" and the slogan.

Lucille Ball portrayed an elderly wealthy widow from Texas. When she was asked if her husband was always rich, she answered, "Nope, born poor and died poor—but when they were digging his grave, they struck oil . . . poor fellow, it took them three days to get his coffin down from that gusher . . . he went greasy but happy." Three quick big howls.

The only continuing character I remember who got laughs week after week with the same morbid subject was on *The Life of Reilly*, both radio and TV. He was Digger O'Dell, Your Friendly Undertaker, played in both mediums by the late comic character actor, John Brown. Digger O'Dell used running gags like, "Remember, always trust your friendly undertaker—he's the last one to let you down." He usually ended his routines saying, "Good-bye, I've got to be shoveling off." This last remark became very popular among listeners and viewers, and many people used it to close conversations.

There have been isolated jokes done on various talk shows, roasts, and situation comedies. They have covered every color, race, and creed. Samples:

Polish: "Did you hear about the Polish widow who has been paying an undertaker $150 a week for twenty years because she buried her husband in a rented tuxedo."

Jewish: Marvin Rosenstein dies in a hospital during surgery and arrives at the Pearly Gates, asking Saint Peter for admission to heaven. Saint Peter looks through his record books and says, "Hmm—today is June 29, 1985—and we have no record showing the death of a Marvin Rosenstein." Marvin says, "Look, I'm dead, or I wouldn't be here." Saint Peter says, "Let me check your name out on the master computer." He presses numerous buttons on a giant computer and suddenly reads: "Ah, here's your name. Marvin Rosenstein. But you weren't supposed to die till 1998. Boy, did you have a *shmuck* for a doctor."

Irish: They were holding funeral services for the late Patrick McMurphy, and his widow and son listened as the priest praised the deceased. Solemnly he said, "Patrick McMurphy was a good husband and father. He was a hard-working man who always brought home his entire paycheck to his wife. Patrick never gambled, chased other women, or drank." At this point the widow leaned over to her son and said, "Go look in the coffin and see if that's your father."

Italian: Anthony's wife died that morning, and his best friend rushed right over to the house to console him, but to no avail. Tony just kept crying, "What I gonna do, what I gonna do, what I gonna do?" Soothingly his friend said, "I know it's terrible, Tony, but time will pass, you'll find another good woman and marry her." Tony sobbed, "I know, but what I gonna do tonight?"

Quaker: Fortitude Williams, the most infamous man in the Quaker community, died suddenly. At the services it is customary for friends and relatives to speak of fond memories of the dearly departed. But no one stood up to eulogize him. After a long embarrassing silence one man rose and said, "Thou all knowest that Fortitude Williams was cheap, mean, stingy, violent, unpleasant, and uncharitable. *But,* compared to his brother Harrison, he was an angel."

It would be easy to list dozens of jokes on death, but as I've said before, jokes are the cheapest commodity in comedy. It's the character and situation that counts. Consider these memorable scenes:

LaVerne (Penny Marshall) follows a good-looking guy into a place that turns out to be an undertaking parlor. She accidentally drops her ring into a funeral urn, reaches in to retrieve it, and then can't get her hand out and spends the next two minutes frantically trying to get rid of the urn without attracting the man's attention.

Or Maud (Bea Arthur) attending the wake of a lady friend, and as she views the body, notices that it is wearing a valuable brooch she had lent the deceased. Like Penny Marshall's antics with the urn, Bea's hilarious efforts at covertly regaining her jewelry were almost all in pantomime.

All in the Family did many death-oriented routines. Once

while Archie was in a hospital awaiting gallbladder surgery, much to Edith's horror and dismay he began giving her instructions on how he wanted her to handle his funeral. It was a laugh-laden routine, during which he said he wanted to be buried in his gray suit, and when she reminded him it was much too tight, he screamed, "Let it out in the back, nobody'll notice it." He also admonished her not to let the undertaker talk her into a satin-lined coffin because "I don't wanna go sliding to the bottom of it."

One show that dealt exclusively with death was called "Stretch Cunningham, Good-bye," and the script was by Douglas Arango, Phil Doran, and Milt Josefsberg.

Stretch Cunningham was the perfect candidate for the coffin. In the early years of the series, Stretch would make an occasional appearance. He had a job with Archie at the loading dock and kept his coworkers laughing with his blue collar bon mots. Though we occasionally talked about Stretch when Archie quoted his latest quip, he hadn't appeared on the show for several seasons, and few viewers would remember him or be upset at his death.

The episode opened with the Bunkers finding out that Stretch Cunningham has died, and the following day Archie can't find his obituary. There is an obituary in the *Daily News*, only it's for a Jerome Cunningham. Archie observes that maybe Jerome was his nickname. Edith says she thinks Stretch was his nickname and Archie grudgingly says, "Maybe you're right, Edith." He looks at the obituary and says, "What the hell is this 'fun serv pend'?" She tells him it means "funeral services pending," and he laments that "Someday we'll open a paper and see behind our names, 'fun serv pend.'" Edith is shaken by this morbid thought, and Archie comforts her by saying, "C'mon, Edith, we all gotta go some time. You today, maybe me tomorrow."

Then to Archie's dismay he is informed that Stretch requested that Archie say a few words at his funeral. Unable to avoid the gloomy chore, he talks Mike into writing a speech for him. He is quite pleased as he starts to read Mike's efforts. "Friends, I have been asked to pay tribute to my good friend Stretch Cunningham. For what is the measure of a man . . . ? He comes into this world torn naked from his mother's womb." Archie turns angrily on Mike. "Am I supposed to say this over the departed remains, to console the dearly departed remainders? 'Torn naked from his mother's womb?' "

Mike snaps back, "Whaddaya want me to say, that he was torn from his mother's womb wearing a tuxedo?"

Archie calms down and asks Mike to rewrite the speech, "and put in somethin' religious even though you don't believe in it. . . . Sprinkle it with some mention of the Lord. Can't you put in some mention of God and Jesus there."

Mike demurs saying he didn't know how religious Stretch was, and Archie screams, "It don't matter if he was religious. He's dead. Dead is the time for religion. You gotta put some Gods and Jesuses in there to let 'em know in Heaven a good man is on his way."

And Mike says, "You mean like making a reservation."

Archie and Mike get into one of their famous biblical arguments, which ends when Archie gets a Bible from the shelf and forces it on Mike, whom he still wants to write the eulogy, saying, "Take it, you atheist. It's the Bible, it ain't a booby trap. Now open it up to the first page. I bet the first thing you see will be good. I only need one little thing."

Mike opens the Bible, peruses it, and says, "You're right, Archie. It says something good on the first page here, like you told me."

Archie asks, "What?"

And Mike reads, "Placed here by the Gideon Society, Property of the Ramada Inn."

The final scene is the funeral, and when Archie enters the chapel, much to his surprise and dismay, he finds that his friend Stretch was Jewish. Trapped, he puts on a yarmulke and stands on the podium above the coffin draped with the flag bearing the Star of David. He takes his speech from his pocket and starts his eulogy. Here is a condensed version of it.

ARCHIE

This here is a little speech I was gonna say, but it's got a lot of mentions of Jesus in it. Not that it's wrong to mention Jesus. After all Jesus was a Jew . . . until his father sat him down and told him no more of that.

REACTION SHOTS OF THE RABBI AND ALL THE MOURNERS THROUGHOUT THE EULOGY.

ARCHIE

And anyway, I don't know if Stretch would wanna go to heaven. It's full of Christians up there, and he might be scared they'd be layin' for him. As we know, they're all angels up there, but you never can tell about human nature. I worked with Stretch, shoulder to shoulder, about eleven or twelve years, so I knew him pretty good. Well, not as good as I thought I knew him. I wish I knew he was Jewish because there was an awful lot of remarks and jokes passed around . . . not by me—some of the other guys. . . . Not that Stretch felt bad. He was an up guy, and was always tellin' jokes. He told Jewish jokes, too. I remember one he told about the priest who said to the rabbi, "Why don't you ever eat ham?" and the rabbi says, "It's against my religion. Why don't you ever go out with a girl?" and the priest says, "It's against my religion," and the rabbi says, "You oughtta try it, it's better than ham." I wouldn't have believed Stretch was a Jew. After all he wasn't a doctor or a lawyer—he was, like me, an ordinary working stiff.

ARCHIE LOOKS DOWN AT COFFIN AS HE REALIZES "STIFF" WASN'T THE BEST WORD TO USE AT A FUNERAL.

I gotta tell you, I was very surprised to find out that Jerome was Jewish. Not that he didn't do an honest day's work. I mean, you couldn't tell from lookin' at his face he was a Jew, and he never showed us nothin' else. I mean, his birth certificate! Well . . . I think I better wind up this urology as fast as I can. I heard somewhere that pain is supposed to take time off your life, so if you laugh, it must have put time on, and Stretch put a lotta time on mine. So I just wish, while you was here, I coulda made you laugh more, Stretch. . . .

LOOKS AT COFFIN.

Jerome . . .

LOOKS AT OTHER END OF COFFIN.

Unless you're at this end.

HE STEPS DOWN OFF OF PODIUM, PASSES BY COFFIN, TAPS IT.

Shalom.

GOES TO EDITH, WHO IS CRYING.

EDITH

Oh, Archie.

ARCHIE

What're you cryin' for, it wasn't that bad?

EDITH

No, it was beautiful!

FADE OUT.

Possibly the greatest episode ever done on death on a comedy series was first aired on the *Mary Tyler Moore* series on October 25, 1975. This high-flown compliment is not just my opinion. It was shared by the National Academy of Television Arts and Sciences, which awarded the 1976 Emmy for Outstanding Writing in a Comedy Series to the script "Chuckles Bites the Dust," written by David Lloyd.

The story started on a serious note. There had been a parade that day, and Chuckles the Clown, who appeared on a children's program on the station Mary worked for, WJM-TV in Minneapolis, marched in the parade in costume. He was dressed as a giant peanut. Unfortunately for Chuckles he was followed in the parade by an elephant. Now it's a fairly well known fact that, when a pachyderm spots a peanut, he instinctively has to shell it and eat it. So the elephant stomped on the peanut, thus ending the life and antics of Chuckles the Clown.

All the habitués of the newsroom, Lou Grant, Ted Baxter, Murray Slaughter, Mary, and others seemed shaken by the unfortunate accident. Then the absolute absurdity of his death struck them. A grown man disguised as a peanut shelled to death by an elephant. One of the men pulled a joke about it, and this unleashed a barrage of boffs, and at each one an indignant Mary got madder and madder. They were unfeeling. Unsympathetic. Cruel. Heartless. The men tried to treat the incident with some dignity, but one after another they'd break into giggles and pull another joke, which made them more hysterical and Mary livid with rage.

The final scene is the funeral. All of the members of the WJM-TV newsroom are there dressed in dark dignity and maintaining an attitude in keeping with the occasion. All seats are occupied by other mourners, friends, and admirers. The minister begins his eulogy extolling Chuckles' virtues as a man, but above all, as an entertainer of children. He then sings Chuckles' childish theme song, and the solemnity of the occasion is broken when Mary gets the giggles over the laughable lyrics. She tries to stifle herself by covering her mouth with a handkerchief. The minister mistakes the muffled sounds for sobbing and asks Mary to give vent to her grief and perhaps say a few words about Chuckles. Mary tries and her efforts, plus the rest of the program, provided viewers with enough laughs to make us realize that the Grim Reaper is, on occasions, not so grim.

So don't be afraid of death—as a subject, not an experience.

V
CHARACTERS, ROUTINES, AND FORMATS
Or: It's Been Done Before

There is nothing more discouraging to the ambitious beginning scripter than the four words, "It's been done before." It's not only true about subjects that everything goes—everything has already went. And when, with finality, a producer concludes a meeting with that fatal phrase, you have been, in the vernacular of veteran writers, "shot down."

But it ain't necessarily so.

True, practically all stories, routines, characters, formats, series have been done before. Your job is to do it better, with a different twist, so that it is salable and enjoyable. What follows is a list of successful ideas which have been done, redone, then revised and done many more times, and each reincarnation has been successful.

Characters

A successful sitcom depends on many equally important ingredients. If you examine the biggest hits over the years, you'll find that they always had clearcut, sharply defined, recognizable characters. *Mary Tyler Moore* had, among others, Lou Grant, Ted Baxter, Mary, and Murray Slaughter. They were aided at various times by Rhoda Morgenstern, Phyllis Lindstrom, Sue Ann Nivens, and others. *All in the Family* had four main players: Archie Bunker, Edith, Mike the Meathead, and Gloria. Lucille Ball had several series and although Gale Gordon did yeoman duty during latter ones, fans most remember the sharply etched original foursome: Lucy, Ricky, Ethel, and Fred. Finally, *The Honeymooners.* There was nothing shaded or obscure in the portrayals of Ralph and Alice Kramden or Ed Norton, and to a lesser degree, Trixie Norton. All the legendary series are as well remembered for their characters as their stories.

Many of today's comedy programs are peopled with players who inherited part of their personalities from those who have graced the airwaves in previous years. In fact, most of the characters that you have laughed at through the years are genetically bound to earlier versions. Let us examine them:

The Wifeless Father

To name a few, he was John Forsythe in *Bachelor Father,* Bill Bixby in *The Courtship of Eddie's Father,* Brian Keith in *Family Affair,* Fred MacMurray in *My Three Sons,* Conrad Bain in *Different Strokes,* and Dolph Sweet in *Gimme a Break.*

On the distaff side we had the husbandless mother with Lucille Ball and Vivian Vance in *Lucy,* in which Lucy played a widow with two children, and Vivian Vance was a divorcée with a son. They shared a house to split expenses. The current hit *Kate and Allie* has two divorcées and their children living together to save money. Lucille Ball's next series was *Here's Lucy,* where she was again a widow with two children, portrayed by her own daughter and son, Lucie Arnaz and Desi Arnaz, Jr. With the passing of Dolph Sweet, *Gimme a Break* continues with Nell Carter fulfilling the role of surrogate mother to the three orphaned girls. (This is probably the only show where a black acts as the parent of white children, although black kids like Arnold [Gary Coleman] and Webster [Emmanuel Lewis] have white adoptive parents.)

The Domestic

This is probably the most successful longest running comedy character in broadcasting. They have been maids, butlers, governesses, valets, and many other callings. They can be any color or sex, but every servant on a sitcom usually has one thing in common with all others. They were always much more knowledgeable than their bosses.

The domestic first appeared in Plautus' plays over two thousand years ago—later reprised in the hit musical and movie, *A Funny Thing Happened to Me on the Way to the Forum.* The longest running and most popular performer in this category was Rochester on *The Jack Benny Show. Time* magazine once said, "Rochester, the sardonic Negro valet, is the granddaddy of all the servants, white and black, who have hilariously put down their employers since the invention of the vacuum tube." And that synthesizes the domestic's duties on a sitcom.

Domestics exploited every facet of comedy. Some were bluntly insulting, like Marla Gibbs as Florence on *The Jeffersons.* Others were sophisticated and suave, like Mr. Belvedere. A partial list of these reliables includes Esther Rolle as Florida on *Maude,* Ann B. Davis as Alice Nelson on *The Brady Bunch,* Shirley Booth as Hazel on *Hazel,* Imogene Coca who, as Grindl, had a different job with a different family or establishment each week. (The *Grindl* show may well be an indication that viewers prefer a group of regular, readily recognizable characters on a steady basis because the series lasted only one season.) Peter Tong on *Bachelor Father,* and, to reverse positions, Susan Blanchard who played the scrutable Occidental housekeeper, Tina, for Pat Morita, the Oriental Mr. T in *Mr. T and Tina.*

The male housekeeper or nanny has been done by others

besides Mr. Belvedere. He was suavely played by Sebastian Cabot as Mr. French on *Family Affair,* and the current hit *Who's the Boss* has Tony Danza playing Tony, a diamond-in-the-rough domestic, working for a lady boss.

Schoolteachers

Several successful shows have been based on teachers. They range from Wally Cox's gentle Mr. Peepers to the trials of Gabriel Kaplan as Gabe Kotter with his Sweat Hogs in *Welcome Back Kotter.* The dignified Ronald Colman as Dr. William Todhunter Hall, president of the college, in *The Halls of Ivy,* and the wisecracking Connie Brooks, delineated by Eve Arden in *Our Miss Brooks.* Bill Cosby was a phys-ed teacher in a series in the early seventies that was called *The Bill Cosby Show* but didn't attain the popularity of the current giant hit of that name. And in the 1985–86 season we had a well-written series, *Mr. Sunshine,* that didn't fare well, probably because viewers didn't like comedy about a blind professor.

Politics

Series based on politics gave us Dan Dailey's Governor Drinkwater in *The Governor and J.J.* and James Noble's Governor Gatling, Robert "Benson" Guillaume's boss in *Benson,* and Benson himself wound up as lieutenant governor. Patty Duke served probably the shortest term in the White House as the first lady President, in a quickly canceled effort, and Kevin Hooks didn't serve a full term in *He's the Mayor.*

Every occupation has been used to garner laughs. We've had cops, soldiers, sailors, cowboys, lawyers, judges, doctors, nurses, and you name it. If you jab a pin into the Yellow Pages of your phone book, chances are it will stab a job that was featured on some comedy program. One notable exception: To this day very few viewers of the popular *Ozzie and Harriet* series can tell you exactly what Ozzie did to support his family and the IRS.

Not only have almost all characters been done before but every facet that made them tick is familiar to viewers. Braggart and wimp. Rich and poor. Sophisticate and innocent. Promiscuous and chaste. Lush and teetotaler. Honest and larcenous. Fastidious and sloppy. Dreamer and realist. Arch conservative and avid liberal.

There are no new characters. Almost all occupations and practically all businesses that could have comic content have been thoroughly explored. Hotels have been done dozens of times. The *Newhart* show is the latest, but Buddy Hackett and Bea Arthur among others did series with inns as backgrounds. Bars were featured on *All in the Family* and its sequel, *Archie Bunker's Place. Cheers'* home is a Boston bar. And in radio, then TV, we had *Duffy's Tavern.* Restaurants were the focal points for *Alice, Three's Company,* and *The Good Guys.* Fictitious television and radio stations were the main locales for fun on *Mary Tyler Moore* and *WKRP in Cincinnati.*

Locked in a Stalled Elevator

The comic possibilities are endless, and writers have continued to take advantage of this with different twists. On the old *Dick Van Dyke* show, he and Mary Tyler Moore found themselves trapped between floors with a crook (played by Don Rickles) who robbed them. Archie Bunker was confined with a group of several people, including a black intellectual and a Puerto Rican woman who gave birth during their imprisonment. More recently, on *Gimme a Break*, Nell Carter and Thelma Hopkins, mad at each other, took adjacent elevators that stalled simultaneously, and they carried on their argument via phones and yelling from their solitary cells.

A variation of this show is Trapped in a Forsaken Spot. This can be a snowbound cabin, or an apartment in a new, unfurnished building deserted for a weekend as Lucy did with Ann Southern and Gale Gordon. Or it can be a cellar where Archie Bunker was in solitary confinement, or a locked storeroom, which Archie Bunker shared with Mike the Meathead.

Why would top-rated shows repeat these shopworn devices? Because the writers came up with brand-new twists that made the old ideas more than palatable.

The Flashback

A standard used by almost everyone. Dick Van Dyke did a memorable flashback when his wife reminded him and some guests how Dick was positive that they brought the wrong baby home from the hospital. They flashed back to a scene where Dick was adamant there was a mixup—after all, in the maternity ward there was another lady with a name similar to theirs who had a baby the same day and the hospital got their flowers and gifts mixed up. Dick phoned the other couple and was mollified when he was told they would drop in to discuss the possible mixup. The couple came—they were black.

All in the Family did an episode where we faded back nine years, to Mike and Gloria's first meeting via a blind date, and it was hate at first sight. They warmed up to each other, and Mike became amorous but Gloria rebuffed him by saying she was a virgin, and he replied in genuine amazement, "Gee, I never met one of those before."

Another variation of the flashback is usually done after a series has been running for several years, and clips of outstanding routines are assembled. Lucille Ball did this, using excerpts from all her previous series. Bob Hope's Christmas shows employ them. Johnny Carson's annual anniversary prime-time program is composed of them. *All in the Family* did two-hour specials commemorating their hundredth and two hundredth episodes. And let's not forget the reunions of yesteryear's popular sitcoms in movie-type programs as done by Andy Griffith's *Mayberry, Gilligan's Island, I Dream of Jeannie, The Brady Bunch* and many others.

The Rashomon Theme

Rashomon is a Japanese film classic in which different witnesses gave their own honest and vastly different dramatized descriptions of the same incident. On comedy shows the same format is followed, where various cast members give widely varying descriptions of the same incident.

Pregnancy

Probably the first sitcom dealing with this delicate condition was not the writer's idea. Desi Arnaz broke the news to them that Lucille Ball was pregnant when *I Love Lucy* was at its height. The writers incorporated this into their scripts. Despite executive misgivings that this was not a suitable subject for comedy, the viewers loved it, and the shows got increasingly higher ratings, culminating with the block buster birth of the baby.

Since then it's been used successfully on many series, including *All in the Family,* where Gloria Stivic's nine months' term was *Reader's Digested* down to four. Sally Struthers (Gloria) was not pregnant, and the prop department supplied her with pillowlike tummies she wore to create successfully the illusion, so that many viewers thought she was actually having a child. Another fictitious baby was born to Ted Knight and Nancy Dussault on *Too Close for Comfort,* but on *Family Ties* they delivered the real thing when Meredith Baxter Birney, mother of the TV "family," decided to have a baby. In real life she doubled her pleasure and had twins, but on the series the producers saved money by limiting her to one.

Hospitals and Doctors

Everyone has had experiences with these, and audiences empathize and laugh at any humor about the inedible food, disappearing nurses, horrendous bills, cold bedpans, and those ridiculous nightgowns you are forced to wear. When

Archie Bunker put one on, he complained, "If you put it on backwards, you're a flasher; if you put it on the right way, you moon the whole world."

Long-Lost Relatives

Missing fathers are very popular. The Fonz was abandoned by his dad as a child, and he was talked about but never seen— except once under mysterious circumstances during which he didn't reveal his relationship. *Happy Days* also did a touching show where the Fonz's half brother, sired by the same peripatetic father, shows up and gives the embittered Fonz a watch left to him by his dad. Of course, the timepiece doesn't work properly, but the Fonz makes his peace with the past when he observes that the watch isn't reliable, but then neither was Pop. . . . On *Cheers,* Cliff (John Ratzenberg), Claven's father, who deserted him, came to the bar to see his son and say good-bye because he was skipping the country to avoid going to jail. Two nights earlier on *Who's the Boss,* Tony Danza's father-in-law, a convict, broke out of jail to visit him.

Brothers and sisters seem almost as popular as fathers in the surprise appearance category. Archie Bunker's brother, a heavy drinker, did several shows. On *LaVerne and Shirley,* Shirley also had an alcoholic brother. In the freshman season (1985–86) of *Golden Girls* they had Rue (Blanche) McClanahan's disliked sister, followed by an episode about Dorothy's equally disliked sister, and eventually Bea's divorced husband showed up. There seems to be a comedy tradition: Long-lost relatives who are heels make for funny programs.

The Law

Involvement with lawyers, trials, and juries keeps cropping up on comedy shows. The comic as a witness or trying to act as a lawyer or serving on juries is an ever popular subject for laughs.

Locales

Practically all have been done before. To a great extent the locale of a series is relatively unimportant, especially if it's a three-camera show. Rarely do shows with live studio audiences use location shots. Archie Bunker and his family lived in Queens, *The Golden Girls* share a house in Miami. *Mork and Mindy* called Boulder, Colorado, home. *LaVerne and Shirley* brewed beer in Milwaukee, but they were done in Hollywood. New York is the habitat of *The Bill Cosby* series, although it's filmed in Brooklyn, and *Kate and Allie* is done in the Big Apple.

The locale of a show rarely lends substance to the series. There are exceptions of course. *Gilligan's Island* depended almost entirely on its complete isolation. Shows have changed locations to derive better subject matter. *Lucy* moved from Danbury, Connecticut, to Hollywood and California for funnier subject matter. *LaVerne and Shirley* started in Milwaukee but several years later they too moved to Hollywood. *Leave It to Beaver* is in the mythical town of Mayfield, and Andy Griffith's series also invented a town, Mayberry. The locale of a series is not important. The contents and characters are.

The Same Story

It happens quite frequently that two different series will have similar themes for episodes within a short time of each other. This is especially true in the late eighties when comedy creators try to be topical. However, it has happened frequently in the past with subject matter that is quite unique, and I'm sure that in the vast majority of cases the writers who did the second version were not consciously copying the first. Examples: In the midseventies on an episode of *All in the Family*, Archie Bunker became infuriated when Gloria and Mike gave his grandson, Joey, a doll to play with. In early 1986,

Michael J. Fox was upset on *Family Ties* when someone gave his baby brother a doll as a gift.

On a *Maude* episode in the midseventies a previously mentioned plot called for a funeral in which Maude tried to retrieve a valuable brooch she had lent the deceased and that was now gracing the chest of the body in the coffin. In 1986, *Kate and Allie* had a mixup through which a woman was being buried in a dress one of the girls had bought and not fully paid for.

In the midsixties, on a *Lucy* program, she phoned her boss feigning illness so she could go to a big sale. She became the one millionth customer to enter the store and was thrilled at the prizes she was to receive till they started to take publicity pictures to publish in the newspapers, and Lucy realized her boss would see them and discover her chicanery. Recently in the reissued *Honeymooners* Ralph Kramden called his boss and claimed he was sick so he could attend a ballgame where he won a car and a thousand dollars. His joy was short-lived when he realized he'd be fired when his boss saw the pictures that would be run in the newspapers. The theme has been done frequently in dramatic shows, usually where a crook is making a getaway from a heist, and he is stopped because he is the ten millionth person to drive through a certain tunnel or cross a bridge.

Occasionally, a series seems to repeat itself, but with good reason. On the *Lucy* show we did an episode where Lucy's boss, Gale Gordon, bought an expensive diamond ring as a surprise gift for his wife. In a moment of weakness he let Lucy try it on. She couldn't get it off, and that was the basis for the entire episode. Some years later, when she was doing the *Here's Lucy* series, Miss Ball was fortunate enough to land Richard Burton and Elizabeth Taylor for a joint guest appearance. The plot here concerned Lucy trying on Liz's ring. *The ring.* Naturally, she couldn't get it off. No plagiarism. When you talked of Taylor and Burton, one topic certain to come up was the size and cost of the diamond. So, with a triple threat of Lucy, Liz, and Burton, plus the multimillion dollar well-publicized ring, we did the show to huge ratings and no complaints.

Series Formats

Will the networks buy a comedy series whose suggested weekly theme has been thoroughly exploited in the past? Yes, especially if the new idea is unique. And if the show it is copying was a huge success, there isn't strenuous objections to a little well-disguised plagiarism.

The most obvious example of TV cannibalizing its hits is found in the family shows. They have been the main staple of situation comedies since the beginning of broadcasting and are far too many to list. Currently (1985–86 season), the runaway ratings leaders are *The Bill Cosby Show* and *Family Ties*. Though they are vastly different from the gentle humor of *Leave It to Beaver*, and *Father Knows Best*, they have the family unit in common. And the problems of the family unit binds them to the abrasive humor of *All in the Family* and *Maude*. As previously noted, there are shows with spouseless fathers or mothers, and programs with adoptive children and surrogate parents. Other series that seem to throw disparate personalities together can be categorized as family shows. In 1979 *The Facts of Life* successfully introduced four adolescent girls with little in common, mother-henned by the housemother of the private school they were attending, and they became sisterlike though they weren't siblings. And six years later, in 1985, while *Facts of Life* was still enjoying prime-time exposure, *The Golden Girls* had practically the same theme, although the four featured middle-aged to elderly ladies dealt with more sophisticated subjects. The family show always was and always will be one of the most viable themes for series.

Will the networks accept another comedy with the military

as its background? Why not? It has frequently worked well. Almost every branch of the service has been the basis for humor. They covered our country's history from the post Civil War's bumbling *F Troop* to the more meaningful *M*A*S*H*, which tackled the touchy subject of Korea realistically and humorously. Prior to the première of *M*A*S*H*, the network was nervous. After its debut some critics were caustic because of its doing controversial comedy about this unpopular war. It was about our misadventures in Korea, and it aired during the Vietnam period. Yet *M*A*S*H* ran longer than any other military oriented program. It received accolades and every possible award numerous times and is enjoying profitable syndication. Other service themed series that had varying degrees of success include Phil Silvers as Sergeant Bilko in *You'll Never Get Rich,* also known as *The Phil Silvers Show, McHales Navy,* and Jim Nabors as *Gomer Pyle.* On the distaff side we had the WAVES in *Broadside* and the WACS in *Private Benjamin.*

What about a show starring an animal that talks? Always good. Most viewers believe that Mr. Ed was the first quadruped who spouted dialogue on the tube. Not so. *The People's Choice,* starring Jackie Cooper, had a basset hound named Cleo who spoke to the audience, but not to the cast. This series was on the air from 1955 to 1958 but *Mr. Ed* didn't utter his first words to Wilbur (Alan Young) Post till 1961. They were both preceded by the big screen's talking mule, *Francis.* All of the animals shared a common speech defect: No one could hear what they said except their masters.

The talking animals became mechanized briefly in 1965 with *My Mother, the Car* when Dave (Jerry Van Dyke) Crabtree bought an ancient secondhand car and was informed by the car's voice that it was a reincarnation of his mother. Of course, no one could hear her but Sonny Boy. Mother's voice was played by a prominent star, Ann Sothern, but this didn't stop *Car* from being junked after one season.

Ghosts

Topper gave us a husband and wife team of apparitions for several seasons. Then came *The Ghost and Mrs. Muir,* which was followed by *Jennifer Slept Here.*

Robots

In the midsixties Robert Cummings was custodian of *My Living Doll,* and in the mideighties there is a syndicated series featuring a prepubescent girl robot in *Small Wonder.* Both of these series were masterminded by writer-producer Howard Leeds, proving that good ideas can always be recycled.

Supernatural Powers

Elizabeth Montgomery made miracles by twitching her nose in *Bewitched,* Sally Fields soared in *The Flying Nun,* and Barbara Eden came out of a bottle in *I Dream of Jeannie,* and caused a network furor over whether lady genies were permitted to show their belly buttons. Years later we had a program about a male genie that ran briefly—maybe because nobody was interested in seeing his belly button.

Visitors from Outer Space

My Favorite Martian first saw the light of night in prime-time in 1963 and ran for four years. In 1978 Mork visited us from the planet Ork, took up residence with Pam Dawber, and we had *Mork and Mindy,* which was an even bigger hit. Both series are rerun regularly. And as of this moment, January, 1987, *ALF,* an alien from outer space who looks like a misbegotten muppet, is a hit on NBC.

The list of familiars goes on and on, so when you are told, "But it's been done before," don't be discouraged. Remember that everything has been done before. Also remember the legendary oft-repeated anecdote that circulated in the industry several years ago: A sparkling new version of the frequently filmed classic *Romeo and Juliet* had a klieg-lighted celebrity-attended première. At its conclusion, as the audience left the theater, one viewer turned enthusiastically to his companion and said, "That was a wonderful movie."

His companion agreed, then added, "Yes, but Shakespeare stole the whole plot from *West Side Story.*"

VI
Writing and Writing with Others

Writers come in all ages, religions, colors, creeds, sexes, intermediate sexes, sizes, and temperaments. Their modes of living and writing habits vary vastly. Some are social butterflies, others practically hermits. Several can only write from midnight to dawn after everyone else is asleep. There are morning writers and afternoon writers. Some write with stereos blasting while others demand deep silence. Some write in shorthand, some in longhand, some will only work on portable typewriters, others use upright electric models. There are those who can only dictate to secretaries. And the newer breed favors the word processor.

There are the pacers, the sitters, the recliners, the nibblers, the eaters, the abstainers, the drinkers, and dozens of other categories. Some can only function in sparsely furnished offices, and others must be surrounded by sybaritic splendor. Some have offices in their homes, and others don't feel at home in their homes. Almost all combine giant-sized egos with psychiatrist-supporting insecurity complexes. A writer can have a program aired on the number one show, have the critics rave about it, and then have his week ruined because his gardener says, "I didn't like last night's show."

Most comedy writers work in teams. A wonderful book describing comedy collaboration is *Act One* by playwright Moss Hart. In one chapter he describes his first day of working with the legendary George S. Kaufman. Hart tells how he is exhuberant and eager to get started, but Kaufman finds endless ways of postponing putting the first words on paper. He sharpens pencils endlessly, adjusts the window blinds, picks lint, real or imaginary, off the rug, straightens his desk, and then sharpens the pencils again and again. Every writer working in tandem knows these various procrastination ploys for avoiding work and has used them. Which is the main reason most of them work with a partner, so that one of them will eventually say, "Okay, let's cut the crap and get to work."

Writers are sometimes categorized for specializing in some special department: "He's great on visual humor." . . . "The tops in topical stuff." This led to a widely quoted anecdote, which wound up on a dramatic show some years ago. The program concerned a comedy series sinking in the ratings, and the two writers had a meeting with the worried network and advertising agency execs. However, every question that was asked by the bosses was answered just by one writer. An exec pointed to the other scribe and said, "Why doesn't he ever answer?" and the first writer explained, "He's the story man."

Each writer needs someone to get him in a working mood. In my capacity as script consultant, story editor and/or producer, I worked solo. But not really. It was my obligation to meet with writers, set stories for shows, then read, criticize, and make suggestions on their first drafts. Eventually I had to rewrite their second drafts when and if needed. After the cast read this second draft, I had to rewrite once again to accommodate the suggestions of the stars and the major cast members. There was also rewriting done during rehearsals, because a scene didn't play well, or a line was needed to cover an actor's entrance or exit.

When I actually wrote scripts, I usually worked with different collaborators. Each one had his own peculiarities and assets. One might be good at visual comedy, another at dialogue. As mentioned, one might have a strong sense of story, another's forte was character. A couple were too easy to please, one was too hard.

New partners need to be handled with finesse. When your new cowriter makes a suggestion that stinks, you tactfully tell him, "I think we can do better." If an explanation and discussion is needed to justify your objection, you do it patiently but not condescendingly. You will find that in the first few days you will each be overly polite. But, if you respect each other's talent, soon after the collaboration begins, you can dismiss a bad suggestion by saying, "That stinks." Time need not be wasted on delicately avoiding hurting each other's feelings.

Teams are always known by their last names. When Mel Shavelson and Jack Rose (graduates from Bob Hope's radio show) were writing, directing, and producing pictures together, an oft-told incident occurred. Mel was in Las Vegas where he ran into his boss, movie mogul Jack Warner, who was with a friend. Warner introduced Mel to his friend by saying, "This is Shavelson and Rose."

Some collaborators have remained together for years, like the teams of Schiller and Weiskopf (*I Love Lucy, Maude, All in the Family*), and Fox and Jacobs (*Lucy, Here's Lucy, Bob Hope*), Madelyn Davis and Bob Carroll, Jr. (*I Love Lucy, The Mother-in-Law, Alice*), and many other teams. Some have lasted less than a day. One of those instant literary marriages lasted less than an hour, and has become a legend among writers.

To avoid embarrassing anyone, and possibly incurring a lawsuit, I have changed their names to Crawford and Walton. A producer suggested teaming up, and they were both willing to give the partnership a tryout, but within minutes Crawford became aware of two major irritants in Walton. First, Walton didn't seem to admire any writer but Walton. Second, he always talked of himself in the third person.

They started by trying to get a story. Crawford made a suggestion. Walton said, "Walton thinks we can do better." Crawford's second suggestion met with, "Walton feels that's too contrived." Crawford tried to launch several other stories, but each time Walton said, "Walton isn't thrilled with that," or "Walton feels that's too hackneyed."

When Crawford had enough, he went to the door and said, "Crawford is going to lunch. Crawford says that if you see Walton, tell Walton that Crawford said 'Walton should go fuck himself.'" End of anecdote. End of collaboration.

Two other incidents are equally famous in comedy writers' history. When the team of Martin and Lewis scored an immediate smash on the tube, no small part of their success was due to a pair of young writers named Norman Lear and Ed Simmons. The scripters had a public relations man, and when they were given several raises, their PR man planted a story in the papers saying that Simmons and Lear were now the highest paid comedy writers in the industry. When Jerry Lewis read this news item, he immediately fired them. His supposed explanation: "If I have to have the highest paid writers, then I'm not funny myself."

The second concerns the previously mentioned team of Schiller and Weiskopf (Bob and Bob), who were the head writers for *The Red Skelton Show*. One morning they were overjoyed to read in the trade papers that the *Skelton Show* was number one in the National Neilsen. Their pleasure turned to amazement when they were fired almost immediately by Red, who explained, "Now that they got to number one they won't work so hard."

Whether a writer scripts solo or with someone else, the best break is to get a staff job. The advantages are obvious: knowing the series' script needs, getting first crack at assignments, etc. The fringe benefit of being on a staff is that you are usually surrounded by bright minds, and in moments of despair you can usually rely on someone to ad-lib a thought that, while not usable, will cause mass hysteria.

Some long-forgotten predecessor once said that every night

group's writing chore always has the Pumpkin Hour. Others call it the Silly Session. There is no special time on the clock when this occurs. It most often happens when writer's block seems to be contagious, and no one can ad-lib anything worthy of the script. Then someone will throw a line that is so utterly unusable or stupid that everyone breaks into hysterical laughter.

One memorable incident occurred during my first season on *All in the Family*. We were rewriting an episode that would be broadcast some weeks after Gloria had given birth to baby Joey. It pivoted on a rather common complaint among new fathers. With the baby in the house, the wife seems to lose all interest in sex. And Michael Stivic was unhappy about this.

From a construction standpoint we knew we were in a fertile field. Our story was based on reality and certainly titillating. In addition to the dialogue based on this friction between Mike and Gloria (and whenever they fought, the results were gratifying), we were sure of two outstanding scenes. First, Gloria would discuss her problem with Edith, then Mike would have a man-to-man talk with Archie. Any kind of sexual discussion involving these characters in any combinations guaranteed pay dirt.

The scene with Edith and Gloria was a breeze. And the one with Archie and Mike flew along packed with lines we knew were surefire. Then the writing got down to Topic A, Mike's complaint. An embarrassed and angry Archie didn't want to go into details of his darling daughter's sexual inhibitions. Angrily he told Mike that when the mood came over him, he should take a cold shower and watch Johnny Carson. Mike answered that he didn't have to get married to watch Carson. Archie asked, "How long have you been married?" "Five years," said Mike. "Well," said Archie, "in those five years you've had more sex than most men get in two lifetimes." So far so good. We were rolling. Now we came to a part that was important to our plot. Archie had to persuade Mike to give up sex for several additional weeks. The speech had to be logical, convincing, and a guaranteed laugh. We thought we had a perfect start. Archie told Mike that there were plenty of men who went without sex. Mike asked who? And Archie's answer was supposed to give three examples—with the third one being funny. (This is an unwritten rule of comedy. Give three examples with the first two setting up the big boff for the third. Comics are leery about doing over three jokes on the same subject. Johnny Carson will occasionally do four or more jokes on a subject, and if the last one just lays there, he'll ad-lib, "Oops, I broke comedy's rule of three.")

Anyway, we sat there, six highly paid, supposedly competent comic minds, and we couldn't get a funny third one. We quickly settled on the two feed lines. Archie would say, "Plenty of men go without sex. Men who are priests. Men in submarines. And men—" But no suitable snapper. We threw line after line with an occasional giggle from someone to show moral support, but nothing that was a roof raiser. We were plodding, punching out pointless jokes, and it was now past midnight. We became listless and our efforts reflected it. Suddenly, one of the group, Larry Rhine, jumped up enthusiastically and said, "I think I've got it." We encouraged him, and Larry broke up the meeting by saying, "Plenty of men go without sex. Men who are priests, men in submarines, and men married to Jewish girls."

We were hysterical. It was the Pumpkin Hour. We knew we couldn't do the line. Five of the six writers were Jewish, and so were our wives. If by one chance in a million the censor permitted us to do it, that meant five celibates who would do without sex for the rest of their lives and even longer. But the hour was late. We were tired. We knew that anything any of us spawned would seem bland compared to Larry's line. We decided to put it in the script, send it to mimeograph, and get some suitable substitute the next day.

The following morning the censor was waiting for us. He

started to scream how *All in the Family* got enough angry mail from minority groups because of Archie Bunker's bigotry. We didn't have to exacerbate the situation by making all our female Jewish viewers mad. Meanwhile, on stage the cast had just read the rewritten script and were wondering whether they could blackmail the Jewish writers on staff by threatening to do the gag. Naturally, we eventually came up with a substitute line. It was fairly good, but it couldn't have been great because I can't recall it.

A couple of additional miscellaneous thoughts on writers. Most people not in the industry haven't the faintest idea of what a writer's function is. I wasn't too surprised to learn that a poll taken some years ago showed that a sizable percentage of viewers in the hinterlands thought they were just visiting with *Leave It to Beaver* or *Ozzie and Harriet,* and observing the actual happenings in those families. I have had people tell me that I have the easiest job in the world, just sitting at my typewriter for half an hour writing a half-hour show. They are amazed to find that it sometimes takes several writers nine, ten, and sometimes twenty hours a day to write those thirty minutes. Almost everyone works nights, and as one writer with prostate trouble said, "We usually work well into the 'wee-wee' hours of the morning."

Strangers aren't the only ones who don't understand exactly what we do. A scripter once observed, "A woman can be married to a writer for fifty years and still not understand that, when she walks into his office and sees him staring out of a window, he is actually working."

Writers understand their own profession, but they frequently attack it from different angles. One basic point we all understand is that we have to start with the best plot or story we can get. Given that and clearcut characters, some shows write themselves. "Write themselves" is a phrase writers use when we are on solid ground, but given all the best ingredients, you still have to add imagination and basic fundamentals. I know writers who claimed to have written a script in less than a day, and they were gems. On rare occasions, when all conditions were right, my collaborator and I have finished a script in two days with laudable results. On other occasions we have sweated two weeks over some scripts that wound up mediocre—although there were some we were proud of.

So now you're doing a script and come face to face with a dry spell. Writer's block. Mental constipation. That's one of the great benefits in collaboration. You always know it isn't your fault, so neither of you think of quitting. Suicide maybe, but not quitting. When I find that we are stuck for a particular joke to service one of the stars so he or she isn't standing on the set like a piece of furniture, I skip it. I come back to it later, but rather than have it louse up the whole day we just go by it. However, and this is important, we only do this when we are positive that we are working with a surefire story.

Remember earlier I wrote about how *All in the Family*'s six-man scripting staff worked for hours over one joke where Archie tells Mike that plenty of men do without sex? How we finally put in an unusable line and called it a night? We didn't shirk our work. We had great scenes with Archie discussing sex with Mike and Edith and Gloria. We knew the rest of the script was larded with laughs. That the line about "marrying Jewish girls" was just something to break up the cast. And we knew that the following day, fresh from a night's rest, we would come up with a good replacement line. Which we did. (That I'll again admit wasn't really great, but it got a good laugh because the audience was rolling at that time.)

So there you have it. The more writers are different, the more they are the same. They procrastinate. They gossip. They think of many inventive ways to forestall the actual writing. But when you come to the basic rules for writing, there is only one to follow. Write!

VII
REJECTION

There is an old saying that there are only two things we can be sure of—death and taxes. Writers can add a third certainty to this—rejection. All creative people are victims of rejection at some time or other, but the good ones eventually enjoy acceptance. Some don't. Vincent van Gogh sold very few of his paintings while he was alive. Personally, I think he cut off his ear so he wouldn't constantly keep hearing the critics say, "That stinks." There is no writer who hasn't experienced this.

However, we all console ourselves with the knowledge that the biggest stars and the highest rated shows in the industry have been turned down more than once. Rejection and frustration are our constant companions. But we can take some small solace in the fact that the biggest names in the business, stars, producers, and all others have met the same setbacks.

NBC's *Bill Cosby Show* was probably the only smash hit of the 1984–85 season and the runaway number one Neilsen show of the 1985–86 season. Yet it was rejected by both other networks. Cosby once said that ABC probably turned the program down because they thought car chases and crashes were more entertaining.

Bob Hope was on five different radio shows for periods never exceeding a single season before he finally clicked on NBC in 1938. And Hope's first movie screen test was nixed by some studio executive whose analysis of the test stated, "His nose seems to come into the scene three minutes ahead of the rest of him."

Bud Yorkin and Norman Lear had to tape *All in the Family* three different times before they finally sold it. When it saw the light of day—or night—as a midseason replacement on January 12, 1971, its low ratings seemed to destine it for a short career. However, CBS decided to air the shows again as summer reruns. Possibly because so few people had caught the original broadcasts, and their curiosity was piqued by all the comment, bad and good, about the series starring a so-called lovable bigot, they tuned in during the hot months, and the ratings zoomed upward. And it led to several other hits including *Maude, The Jeffersons, Sanford and Son, Mary Hartman, Mary Hartman,* among others.

Before Carroll O'Connor, who became the highest paid performer on a weekly series, was selected to head up the cast of *AITF,* Mickey Rooney was considered for the Archie Bunker role and was given the script to read. Rooney is reputed to have told the producers he'd do the show if they changed the leading role to that of a blind detective with a Seeing Eye dog. (And Debbie Reynolds, not Jean Stapleton, was the original choice for Edith Bunker.)

Carroll O'Connor wound up with what may be the role most indelibly etched into the minds of viewers, but Carroll himself has known rejection. Prior to TV he was an excellent though not starring dramatic actor on the stage and in films. He played an important part in *Cleopatra,* but most of us were too busy watching Elizabeth Taylor's cleavage to notice anyone else. In early 1964 he was flown from New York to Los Angeles to try for a featured role in a new series. But the results were negative, and Carroll didn't get to play the Skipper on *Gilligan's Island.* Alan Hale, Jr., did very well in that role.

And *Gilligan's Island* itself brought an assortment of rejections to its writer and creator, Sherwood Schwartz. Sherwood left a lucrative position as Red Skelton's head writer to devote his time to creating a comedy series. His first successful brain-child was *Gilligan's Island*, but before it debuted on the air, he suffered several kinds of rejection.

There was interest in Schwartz's series idea from the start, and he had many meetings with the then head of CBS, James Aubrey. Aubrey was efficient, but his cold dealings with creative people won him the sobriquet "the Smiling Cobra." At one of the conferences, Aubrey suggested that Sherwood change the concept of his show so that it revolved around a charter boat available for fishing or sightseeing every week. Although Schwartz was anxious to sell his series, he wanted it to be *his* series. He envisioned *Gilligan's Island* as a small microcosm of civilization. Further, he felt that by having them cut off from the world, without automobiles, new clothing, and other modern conveniences, the series would never look dated in reruns. (He was right. *Gilligan's Island* has probably been the tube's most rerun series since the late sixties, and because of its locale it still has a today look. Garry Marshall was also a great believer in this because two of his most successful series, *Happy Days* and *LaVerne and Shirley*, although achieving their success in the seventies and eighties, were locked in time in the late fifties or early sixties, so their clothes, automobiles, etc., are always in acceptable style.)

Sherwood was adamant in sticking to his guns and held out for the series dealing with castaways on an island. Aubrey was also adamant, and probably to show Sherwood he was wrong, he put a series called *The Bailey's of Balboa* on the network. It starred Paul Ford, who ran a small charter fishing boat, and was based on Aubrey's idea. Possibly to take the edge off Sherwood's series, *The Baileys of Balboa* was scheduled to air its first program on September 24, 1964, just two days ahead of *Gilligan's* debut. However, *The Bailey's* never made an impact on the public, lasted one season, and is long forgotten. *Gilligan's Island* enjoyed a three-year career and today, nearly twenty years later, it is one of the darlings of the independent stations, some of which rerun it as often as two and three times daily.

One of our best loved series, often held up as a hallmark of quality in performance and writing, is the original *Dick Van Dyke Show*. The pilot was conceived and written by Carl Reiner. Carl had been one of the strongest performers, and a contributing writer, on the Sid Caesar shows. Reiner conceived this idea, which featured a trio of writers preparing programs for a comedian, based loosely on his own experiences, and Carl hoped to portray the leading character. The immediate reaction to the pilot script was happiness and hosannas, with one teensy weensy objection. The powers that be felt that Carl Reiner wasn't the type to play the part of Rob Petry, the character who was based on Carl Reiner. So they hired Dick Van Dyke, and while probably Carl's initial reaction was rejection, I'm sure that in retrospect he feels no sorrow.

The first time I faced rejection was in the midthirties when I was a very young press agent trying to become a writer. I, and two press agent friends, Sid Garfield and Eli Lloyd Hoffman, were introduced to a comedian who was to appear in the stage show at the Capitol Theater, and he wanted some topical jokes and some fresh ones to brighten up some routines he used in his act. Oh yes, the comedian's name was Bob Hope.

The three amateur scribes met early one evening after we had finished our publicity work and proceeded to write the best we knew how. The following evening, eager and anxious, we took our six-page joint offering over to Bob. He read it, making complimentary comments on many of the lines. I don't remember which of us wrote what, but I clearly recall his reaction when he came to one of my contributions. A joke to fit into a bit he did about a crummy nightclub. The line, and I remember it roughly, was "And you should see the orchestra there. This was the first time I ever saw an orchestra leader conduct a band by waving a salami." Hope smiled as he read it and then said, "That's a very funny joke." Elation on my part. Then Bob added, "I always laugh at it when I hear Georgie Jessel tell it." The depths. Not only rejection but the very first comic I ever worked for told me I stole gags. I protested saying that I would never hand him someone else's jokes. Bob said, "I believe you. I've read lots of funny gags under your name in Walter Winchell's column. I don't think you steal jokes even though your name is Milton." (The last remark was a friendly barb at a contemporary of Bob's who was then noted for stealing other comic's jokes—Milton Berle. Bob wasn't knocking Berle by saying this, nor am I by printing it. Berle capitalized on his reputation as the Thief of Bad Gags, and joked about it himself by saying of a fellow funny man, "His act was so funny I laughed so hard I dropped my pencil.") Oh, yes, Bob liked our material so much that he paid us $50.00, and this was big brackets for just one night's work; $50.00 was a princely sum in those days, even split three ways.

We went to see Bob when he opened at the Capitol Theater, and he went over big. Even our material sounded great. We went backstage; I pretended that the rejection of my Georgie Jessel joke never happened. We told Bob that whenever he did something that needed writers, please remember us. A couple of years later Bob signed for a new radio series that would originate far from our homes, in California. My two collaborators were reluctant to leave their life in New York. I was hesitant too, because by this time I had built a reputation as a press agent, was making over a hundred dollars a week, and had a bright young man, a Cornell graduate, working for me and paying him $17.00 per week. He became my new collaborator. Mel Shavelson.

When Shavelson and I joined Bob's writing staff, rejection was the rule, but in a way that rarely hurt anyone's feelings. Each writer or team turned in a full script each week. The teams' efforts were allowed to be 50 percent longer than the single scripter's. Bob then read each script and marked a single check on every joke he liked at first glance. A second reading resulted in an X being marked on the checked lines he still liked. The third and final reading found him circling the X'd checks, and these were the jokes he wanted put in the first draft of the scripts, which were assembled by various teams of writers. Whether Hope truly liked everything he initially read, or whether he always wanted his writers to feel confident, is a moot question. The fact is, in each writer's script practically every single joke got the preliminary check mark of approval.

One of the rejections I remember most came during the first program I worked on for Jack Benny. The writers at that time, besides myself, were George Balzer, John Tackaberry, and Cy Howard. Sam Perrin joined us two weeks later. We had written our first draft of our first script and were now having our first rewrite session with Jack in his penthouse suite at the Sherry-Netherland. Our progress was fairly smooth till we reached one spot that Jack felt needed a different and better line. We took turns ad-libbing lines but to no avail. After several minutes I threw one that broke up everybody, including Benny. It was the first time I had made Jack laugh, and I gloated silently. Later I was to learn that Jack was the easiest laugher in the business. He would laugh and fall on the floor. And frequently roll on it. Some years later we were talking about Jack's propensity for falling to the floor, and George Balzer said, "If a writer doesn't cause Jack to send a suit to the cleaners twice a week, he's not earning his money."

The laughter, which lasted rather long, much to my delight, subsided, and Jack said, "Okay fellows—we still need a line for that spot." I, and all the writers, were surprised at this because of the reaction my ad-lib got. So I asked, "Jack—what about the line I just threw?"

Jack looked at me and said, "But, Milt, that was a *joke!*"

We all realized what Benny meant. I had said the line like a stand-up comedian, and it did sound rather jokey. From that incident we all learned that Jack would accept jokes only when their wording didn't sound like jokes.

One of the legendary yarns concerning how writers deal with rejection is about an old friend of mine who has been in the business as long as I have, is close to my age, and also keeps working steadily. Harry Crane. Harry has a long list of credits and was one of the creators of Jackie Gleason's *Honeymooners.* And this anecdote deals with Crane and the great Gleason. It was well over a quarter of a century ago, and Gleason was doing a variety show. The blackout on one of the sketches seemed weak to him so he sent the writers to their offices to come up with a better one.

Some time later each staff member returned and told his idea to Gleason, and all were automatically shot down. Crane entered a bit later explaining his tardiness by saying something like, "Jackie, I know it took me a little longer but what I have is worth it. It's probably the funniest line of the season."

Jackie said, "Read it."

Crane continued, "Before I do, I must tell you that I'm surprised that such a great gag should come from me—it's worthy of Mark Twain."

Gleason again said, "Read it."

Once more Crane extolled the virtue of his creation, "The only thing that worries me about this joke is that the audience will scream so loud and long that the vibration of their laughter could cause the ceiling to fall on them. It's doubtlessly the best joke in history."

And again Gleason said, "Read it."

Harry read it.

Gleason said, "I don't like it," and without a moment's hesitation Crane said, "I got a better one." And he did. Jackie liked his second offering.

Whether Crane was kidding Gleason with his first joke, or whether, like William Tell, he had a second arrow in his quiver, he persisted, and that's what every writer must learn to do.

Possibly the most expensive mass rejection of upper echelon writers came in 1979 when NBC, via Fred Silverman, ordered about thirty comedy pilots at a cost of over $20 million. Not one was made into a series.

Like others I learned that there isn't always finality in rejection. In the late 1950s I created a series centered around a business called the Unique Employment Agency—Odd Jobs for Odd People. There was mild interest, but since I was gainfully employed at the time I didn't pursue the project.

In 1968 I had served four years as script consultant on the *Lucy* series, which was in its sixth year on the air, when Miss Ball announced she wanted to do a new series. I remembered my old idea, rewrote it with Gale Gordon owning the agency and Lucy playing his widowed sister-in-law, going out on most of the odd jobs.

The new series went on the air as *Here's Lucy,* ran for six years, and was frequently rated number one and was almost always in the Top Ten, a tribute to Miss Ball's talents rather than my idea. It did very well for me as I collected royalties, writing fees, and a regular salary plus residuals on each of the aforementioned.

So writers, remember two things: Never throw anything away, and learn to live with rejection. It goes with the territory.

VIII
CRITICS

There is a widely quoted joke in the industry: "Asking a writer what he thinks about critics is like asking a lamppost how it feels about dogs." And while I'm quoting anticritic cracks, one of the most famous is, "Critics are like eunuchs in a harem. They see it done every night, and they're mad because they can't do it themselves."

There are critics in every creative field. Possibly the most powerful are the theatrical critics. A bad review in the *New York Times* is tantamount to a closing notice. Yet there have been noted exceptions. The 1920s play *Abie's Irish Rose* had a long running, money-making career despite almost unanimously scathing reviews in the New York dailies. *Hellzapoppin'* seemed headed for an early curtain but columnist Walter Winchell began plugging it daily till it became a hit.

Movie and TV reviewers don't carry the clout of critics of the New York theater. In the theater the show opens one night, it's reviewed in all papers the following morning, and that afternoon there are long lines of ticket buyers or a closing notice posted, depending on what the reviews said. Movies are reviewed in different cities on varying dates (depending on when they open) and don't have the mass impact. TV shows are usually reviewed on their opening programs, and since not too many viewers in the smaller cities and towns read reviews, they are not an enormous influence. This is one of the reasons why the overnight Neilsens taken in large cities some-times are at great variance with the National Neilsens.

Also, there is seldom the unanimity of opinion among TV critics that seems to be shared by the theatrical critics. Per-haps this is because in the theater the critics all see the same show the same night and are influenced by the audience's and their fellow critics' reactions.

Pleasing critics is a difficult assignment. You never know what they want, and frequently they're not sure themselves. Many years ago John Crosby, who reviewed radio for the *New York Herald-Tribune*, devoted his entire column to a rave about the previous night's Jack Benny broadcast and lavishly praised the writers. He sent the review to Mr. Benny with a request for a script of the show. Some time later he wrote another column referring to the first ecstatic review. He said that he read the script and that the writing was dull and flat. He may have been right. Scripts are not meant to be read—they are to be performed. "Well, excuuuuuuuuse me," and "Can we talk?" are not laugh-provoking when you read them, but when said by Steve Martin and Joan Rivers, you do smile or laugh.

Benny's writers, who were so overjoyed by the first review, brooded about the follow-up comment. We discussed taking ads in the trade papers, running the columns side by side and asking, "Which John Crosby can you believe?"

We did nothing because in the industry you quickly learn that feuding with critics is a no-win war. The critic invariably has the last word.

A classic example took place well over half a century ago. A theatrical critic (I believe it was Heywood Broun) not only destroyed a show with his review but devoted most of it to lambasting an actor whom I will call William Wister. Broun said, in effect, "William Wister is the worst actor in the world. If he were a butcher, he'd be the world's worst butcher." The disparaging remarks went on and on and stigmatized and defamed Wister to such an extent that he brought suit for libel and/or slander and/or defamation of character. He won a tiny token award.

A year passed, and once again William Wister appeared in a legitimate show, and Broun was there on opening night to cover it. The following morning everybody in the industry immediately turned to the theatrical section of their papers to read Broun's review. He devoted much space to his comments about the play, the scenery, the lighting, the acoustics, and all the performers, excepting one. He did not mention William Wister until his last line, which read, "William Wister's performance was not up to his usual standards."

In television comedy the writers seem to be the critics' favorite target. First to be blamed, last to be praised. One critic who was friendly with Red Skelton couldn't bring himself to rap Red. So if he panned or praised the program he almost always said, "Red rose above his material again." One of Skelton's writers complained, "Hasn't he ever seen Skelton fall below his material?"

I was once amazed to read a squib somewhere saying that while Lucille Ball's scripts were funny, they weren't in the same class as Noel Coward's plays. True. But if Lucy's scripts were like Coward's plays, there's scant chance she'd have ruled the ratings for all those years. They were aimed at her specific audience.

Occasionally, irrelevant emotions color the comments of reviewers. A writer who was quite friendly with a critic was shocked to read his column on a sitcom episode he had written, which was pure vitriol. The writer was a veteran, quite objective about his work, and felt that not only wasn't the program bad, but it was quite clever. After hearing from coworkers that they too thought the write-up unfair, he called the critic. This gentleman immediately agreed with him. The program really wasn't that bad, but just before he watched it, he had a rhubarb with his wife and was in a vile mood. The writer told friends about this and added, "I know how he made up with his wife. He did the same thing to me."

So you can get a bad review because of a domestic tiff. Also as the result of a touch of indigestion, an IRS audit, a nasty nick while shaving, a dented fender, a dog messing on the rug, a leaky roof, an overdue mortgage payment, a child's bad report card, a gravy stain on a new tie, constipation, a lousy golf game, a decline in the stock market, hemorrhoids, or— heaven forbid—because you wrote a lousy script.

Most reviewers are fair, but they do make mistakes. When Mary Tyler Moore's show first saw the light of day—or night —in 1970, I was working for Lucille Ball. Lucy and I both viewed the opening program and discussed it objectively. We loved it. I was surprised when a few days later a prominent national news magazine made short shrift of it with a somewhat derogatory paragraph saying it had no future. Several years later, when the series did its final episode, this same magazine devoted a full page to it, saying that it was doubtless one of the greatest programs ever to hit the air. This is not the sole example. Many shows that are now regarded as classics started with lukewarm press receptions, and many critics who originally dismissed these programs realized on further viewing that they had made a mistake and gave second and more glowing opinions. Unfortunately, sometimes these mistakes can discourage viewers and curtail the growth of a potential giant.

The longer you're in the business, the better you know how to handle press notices. The good ones find their way into your scrapbook—the bad ones wind up in the fireplace. But you've got to expect the occasional slings and arrows, barbs and bites. You leave yourself open to sulfuric statements about your efforts the moment you put pen to paper professionally. A famed novelist once said, and I paraphrase his statement, "If you can't stand criticism, don't become a writer. Be an obstetrician. Nobody has ever said to an obstetrician, 'You call *that* a baby? It needs more work. Give me something better.'"

IX
CENSORSHIP

Censorship has been the bane of writers since papyrus and the alphabet were invented. Probably even before. Some ancient scribe must have had his hieroglyphics scraped off a tomb because it was decided he told too much truth about the monarch resting there.

Writers in radio, movies, and television constantly wage war with the wielders of the blue pencils. Fortunately, most censors have a good sense of humor, and you can reason with them. One such executive—and the networks refer to his department as the Continuity Acceptance Office—used to send out an occasional newsletter printing the most interesting complaints he received. One concerned a glamorous girl who was a regular on a panel show and was noted as much for her ample chest as for her wit. She emphasized her physical assets by wearing the lowest cut gowns allowable. On one occasion she leaned forward, an event which caused coast-to-coast gulping. The letter concerned this incident, and its final sentence went, "All I can say is that either that dress was cut too low or that girl is built too high."

But that was years ago when practically every program was done live, and it was impossible to delete something ex post facto. Currently, situation comedies are filmed or taped, and the censors can, and do, cut. It is the duty of the writer to see that nothing important that furthers the action is excised. Jokes, maybe, plot never.

There are tricks of the trade in doing this. The most common way to save something that is borderline but important is to include two or three obviously objectionable lines. You put up strenuous arguments to save all the lines, then compromise, get rid of the few you had no intention of including, and save the one you need. There's a drawback to this. Sometimes the writer puts up too good an argument and saves the decoys along with the wanted one. The normal procedure is to wait a while, call the censor, and tell him you've been thinking it over, and he may have been right, you'll cut another offending speech. This is like winning a double header, because you keep the line you want and convince the censor you're a reasonable person.

Possibly the biggest brouhaha ever to arise from impending censorship came prior to the 1939 filming of *Gone with the Wind.* They refused to let Clark Gable, as Rhett Butler, make his exit by telling Scarlett O'Hara, "Frankly, my dear, I don't give a damn." It became a national imbroglio. Editorials were written about it. A few felt that hearing the word "Damn" spoken by our number one box office star would lead to gross immorality among moviegoers. The majority of newspapers felt that the line fit the situation, and Clark could hardly exit by saying, "Frankly, my dear, I don't give a hoot" . . . or darn. Both "hoot" and "darn" were suggested alternatives, but "damn" won, and the U.S.A. did not sink into depravity. Today there would be no questions asked if he made his exit saying, "Frankly, my dear, I don't give a four-letter word." (Fill in your own.)

Occasionally, writers realize that they have something censorable, but they call on clever subterfuge and get away with it. When the boisterous Hecht-MacArthur newspaper play, *The Front Page,* was sold to movies, everyone wondered how they would get away with the wonderful, risqué blackout of the stage show. In the play, Hildy Johnson was the star reporter on a Chicago daily, working for a ruthless editor named

Walter Burns. Johnson wants to go to New York to get married, and Johnson uses every stratagem to get him to stay in the Windy City. Finally, the editor warmly bids good-bye to the reporter, wishes him well, and insists on giving him a gift, a wristwatch that was presented to him by some admirers. Johnson protests he can't take the watch; after all, it was valuable, both sentimentally and intrinsically. The back of it was engraved, "To Walter Burns," plus some flowery phrases. Burns insists that he wants Johnson to have it, and he better hurry or he'll miss his train. Johnson exits after an almost tearful good-bye. There is a pause as the pensive editor seems to think affectionately of his lost reporter. He goes to the phone, calls the police and says, "This is Walter Burns. Stop the Twentieth Century Limited and arrest Hildy Johnson. The son of a bitch stole my watch." Curtain to one of the biggest and best blackouts ever seen on the Broadway stage.

In 1931 it was made into a movie. There was no question about saying "son of a bitch." The Hays Office, official industry watchdog, would never okay the picture's release. But they circumvented the censors and still retained the essence of the blackout. Adolphe Menjou played the editor, Walter Burns, and Pat O'Brien was the star reporter, Hildy Johnson. The blackout followed the stage play exactly except for one minor detail. At the end, as Menjou called the police, he was sitting at a desk with his elbow resting on an upright typewriter. As he came to the offending epithet, his elbow hit the carriage, which slithered across the typewriter making a buzzing noise, and, while you could see Menjou's lips form the words "son of a bitch," you never heard the offending phrase.

The networks don't seem reluctant about showing Walter Matthau starring in one of the last remakes of the picture enunciating the phrase clearly. And on a *Maude* episode Bea Arthur clearly mouthed the same words, so there is no mistaking her meaning.

Pregnancy was a frightening word to television's guardians

of our tender morals. While they permitted dramatic shows to say "pregnant," comedy shows had to use euphemisms.

When Lucille Ball became pregnant in the early 1950s and the writers incorporated this into the series, CBS had a priest, a minister, and a rabbi scan the scripts so there would be nothing that might offend anybody. In an article some years ago in *TV Guide,* written by Maurice Zolotow, Lucy talked about the episode where she gave birth. "It was a good show, human and funny. But we received many letters denouncing us for being obscene. Some folks thought it was bad taste to show a pregnant woman on television. Today they not only show you pregnant women on television, but they show you how they got that way."

During all her shows prior to the program on which she gave birth to Desi, Jr., never once was the word "pregnant" used on the air. Compare this to the 1975 *All in the Family* episode, written by Hal Kanter, where Gloria and Mike announce to Edith and Archie that she is pregnant.

Archie shushes her, "Don't say that word, it sounds like you did something dirty."

Mike says, "We did."

Archie remonstrates again, and Edith sides with him saying, "In my day we used to say anticipating a bundle from heaven."

Archie adds, "Or you could say you're expecting a visit from the stork."

Mike asks, "How do you feel about 'knocked up'?"

Continuity Acceptance made a token objection to the phrase, but we got away with it.

The conniptions caused by the word "pregnancy" were minor to the arguments that erupted when we tried to do humor on preventing pregnancy. Writers soon learned that they had a viable argument when they did a joke that seemed to imply contraception, and then added a line that showed our intentions were strictly honorable.

Here's Lucy did a show where Lucy was taking dictation

from Jack Benny at his home. The doorbell rang, admitting George Burns and two cute looking seventy-five-year-old ladies, the boys' dates. One of the elderly ladies said, "Jack, sorry to be late, but we had to stop at the drugstore to pick up the Pill." Amazed, Lucy asks, "The pill?" And Burns answers, "Yes, the one that keeps us awake."

An *All in the Family* episode faded back to how Mike and Gloria first met—a blind date. As Mike and his pal start to leave to meet the girls, his friend said, "We've got to stop at the drugstore to get something to take the worry out of being close."

With a delighted expression Mike asked, "What do we have to get?"

And his friend answered, "Clorets."

The above bits were done on CBS, and the censor objected dutifully but lost both battles. First, he was arguing with three giants, Benny, Ball, and Burns. In the second case he was battling with the Neilsen's number one show.

But birth control evidently didn't bother CBS too much several years later when *The Mary Tyler Moore* series did an episode where her parents were visiting. One night her dad had a cold, and Mary was going on a date with a man. Her mom, obviously talking to her sick spouse, said, "Don't forget to take your pill," and Mary and her dad answered simultaneously, "I will."

Contraception is an occasional topic for both serious and comic conversations on the late night talk shows. Several years ago they were discussing the efficiency and reliability of oral contraceptives, and one guest said, "Ladies have always had the most effective oral contraceptive: 'No.'"

The fart has been used for centuries by literary giants from Boccaccio to Mark Twain, who privately printed a pamphlet on the art of the fart in Medieval England. Some years ago the movies discovered audiences would laugh at this, and we saw an elderly lady in *10,* and the running gag was that practically everyone of her moves was accompanied by a rumbling breaking of wind. Mel Brooks' *Blazing Saddles* had a low comedy, but highly hysterical, scene showing a group of cowboys dining on beans, and dialogue was soon replaced by a well orchestrated fugue for farts. In the hit picture *Cocoon*, a senior citizen accepts his daughter's invitation to dine out by saying, "Okay, but not Italian food, it makes me fart."

Television always follows the lead of pictures, and jokes about farts that were soon seen, or at least heard, on the tube. Archie Bunker did one where he came home complaining that the guy standing next to him on the subway train had beans for lunch. When Edith asks how he knew, Archie replied, "Because he was the only one on the train smiling." And when one of his friends was admiring his month-old grandson in his crib, we heard a tiny popping sound, and the friend said, "He just burped." Archie sniffed the air and said, "That was no burp."

On a cable TV show Bill Cosby hilariously discussed his father as a farter. One line tells how when his seated father breaks wind he rises several inches above his chair.

Censors have cut big laugh lines that probably would have offended very few. When Elizabeth Taylor and Richard Burton appeared on *Here's Lucy*, Gale Gordon bragged to Burton that at the all-male college he attended, he played the part of Cleopatra in *Anthony and Cleopatra*, and he was sensational until the suicide scene where he tripped on the snake.

Burton asked, "You mean, you fell on your asp?"

It was corny, but having a star of Burton's stature say it made it funny. It was never broadcast because the censor thought it too naughty. However, a few years later all networks, including CBS, ran a major gasoline company's commercial that had the catch phrase, "If you're not getting good mileage, your car needs a kick in the gas."

The longest and most bitter fight my colleagues and I ever had with the censors was the battle over frontal nudity. In

January 1976 we did an episode where Archie baby-sat for his month-old grandson Joey. We thought we had a cute and touching scene where the gruff grandfather lovingly performed the distasteful chore of a much needed diaper change. The censor said, "No go. You're showing Joey naked from the waist down. That's Male Frontal Nudity."

We argued that the child was small and would be tiny on the TV screen and his genitalia would be infinitesimal. The censor was adamant. So were we. The scene was not only tender, tinged with humor, but it was vital to our story, so we had to resort to a power we rarely used. Norman Lear.

Reinforced by Norman, we met again with the censor. He grudgingly gave ground. He would okay the scene if Archie diapered the baby while little Joey was lying on his tummy. To our amazement Lear seemed to agree with him.

Norman said, "Sure, we'll do it that way—if you can show us one mother in the world who diapers her baby face down."

An embarrassed pause. A capitulation. And for the first time in history America was exposed to Male Frontal Nudity on TV. We never got one letter of complaint.

So much has changed over the years. On *The New Dick Van Dyke* show in the early 1970s, they filmed an episode where Dick and his wife had a discussion with their preteen daughter on making love, who the previous night had walked into their bedroom and glimpsed the couple in the act. Because Carl Reiner was in charge of the series, the program was done in the best of taste. But nobody ever knew. CBS refused to air that episode. However, in the 1984–85 season, *Webster* did an episode where Webster walked in on his adoptive parents in the same situation. They explained, in terms he could understand, that they were displaying affection for each other. Later in the program Webster gets into trouble because the mother of a friend of his, a girl, found him and her daughter in the nude. A far cry from a dozen years ago, and an even farther cry from the famed act of censorship that clipped a sequence from a special because white Petula Clark touched the arm of black Harry Belafonte. You see, Webster is black—the little girl was white.

Today, we have cable programs like *Good Sex* with Dr. Ruth Westheimer, who could pass for anybody's favorite grandmother, talking about condoms, IUD's, premature ejaculation, oral sex, and "make sure the penis is moist before inserting it into the vagina." Problems with the censors are dwindling fast.

X
THE SITUATION COMEDY
The Creative and Technical Aspects

The dream of every comedy writer is to create a series that runs four or more years. This gives him an opportunity to develop lasting characters, write funny scripts, do public service programs, and make a hell of a lot of money on reruns.

There are two major kinds of sitcoms: hard comedy and soft comedy. *All in the Family* became the king of hard comedy immediately after its debut, and though off prime time for several years, it still retains the crown. Soft comedies were ruled by shows like *Father Knows Best, Leave It to Beaver,* and others.

The hard shows go for guffaws instead of giggles. They tackle topics that were discussed only at sophisticated private gatherings a score of years ago. Michael Stivic's temporary impotence was the basis for an entire early episode of *All in the Family,* and when Archie tried to explain the Meathead's sexual problem to a fellow bar habitué, he said, "He can't get it out of neutral." A far cry from an early family-type soft sitcom where a son asked his father for an erector set for Christmas, and the censor changed it to Tinkertoy because erector sounded suggestive.

Shows in the hard comedy category don't necessarily deal in controversy. All of Lucille Ball's series were hard because they went for the big laughs, not the smiles. Many others, such as *The Honeymooners,* never tried for subjects more stimulating than "Will Alice keep Ralph on his diet till he loses weight?" But they were always ambitious in their depiction of real-life characters and situations faced by the vast majority of their viewers. Soft series dealt with "How will David or Ricky raise $2.50 to buy an orchid for the Senior Prom?" They were content with chuckles and smiles rather than screams and memorable moments.

Most hard shows are filmed in front of live audiences, using several cameras simultaneously. Series using only one camera, with scenes shot movie-style out of sequence, are frequently soft.

I Love Lucy was one of the first, if not the first, to film in front of a live audience. It used what became known as "the three camera" technique (because some genius pointed out that these shows were filmed with three cameras). The programs were presented to audiences like short stage plays, completely in sequence, with three cameras simultaneously focused on the action. One camera usually was used for a "master shot"—showing the entire set and all the performers. A second camera might be devoted to an extreme closeup of the performer whose actions were most important at the moment. The third camera usually was used for a "two shot"— a semicloseup of the two principals most involved at that specific second. The audience in the studio saw the scene as it unfolded, and laughed at the action and dialogue, all of which was duly recorded on the sound track. Actors frequently flubbed lines, and then the director used his discretion as to stop the scene and start again from the top, or to continue and pick up a shot of that particular line or bit after the audience departed. The three-camera technique has its advantages. The actors hear the audience reaction, and they react to the reaction, frequently giving more spontaneous and sparkling performances. The laughter, applause, and other audience acts of approval is honest, although, as mentioned, occasionally "sweetened." The performers, producers, writers, and directors have an instant assessment of their efforts, and this can give a valuable insight as to what their viewers will accept and appreciate most readily.

There are also disadvantages in using the so-called three-camera live technique. Because of studio space restrictions, you can only write in a limited number of sets. Look at reruns of past hits, and you'll see *All in the Family, Dick Van Dyke, LaVerne and Shirley,* and a host of others confined their comedics to three sets, sometimes squeezing in a fourth. *Barney Miller* and *Taxi* usually used one basic set, although *Barney Miller* had an adjoining small office. *Cheers* confines its action to the bar and occasionally the private office.

Location scenes are verboten. You can't show anything that depends on camera tricks, such as fast and slow motion. Forget about writing magical stunts where vases float in air or things disappear, which were commonplace in the gimmick shows. (*Bewitched, I Dream of Jeannie, The Flying Nun, My Favorite Martian,* among others.) These were all filmed with one camera, no audience, and fall into the soft comedy class.

Don't even think about auto chases, trains, or planes, and large outdoor scenes. You may see them occasionally in three-camera shows, but they are stock shots. Stock shots are what the name implies. For instance, if Bill Cosby had to meet a friend at the airport, you would probably see a living room scene ending with Cosby leaving his house. Then there would be a shot of JFK airport and planes landing or taking off. Next we would see the set of the airport area where Cosby had to meet his friend, specially constructed in the studio and peopled with extras and actors. They would do the scene where Bill meets his friend, and they leave. Next we might see a cab pulling up to the exterior of the Cosby house, already established via a frequently used shot on almost every episode they did. Next we would show the living room interior and have

Bill and his friend enter. Cosby has never left the studio but by inserting the stock shots the viewers get an impression of greater scope and mobility.

Although almost all shows done before live audiences can be classified as hard comedy, it doesn't follow that all of those that used the one-camera technique sans spectators were soft comedies. The old beloved *Phil Silvers Show* and *Car 54, Where Are You?* and the more recent *M*A*S*H* are prime examples of hard comedy series done without audiences.

The one-camera programs are filmed exactly the same way movies are made. The script is usually shot out of sequence. If the program uses several sets, they will shoot all scenes that take place in the living room, one immediately after the other. Next, if there are two scenes in the bedroom, they will shoot these. If there are three scenes in the kitchen, these will be done, etc. Sometimes when one set is finished, it is "re-dressed" to resemble another new set and then used again. Finally, in the editing room, the scenes are routined in continuity.

The three-camera show caters to the studio audience and is shot in exact sequence so the viewers can follow the story. For instance, on the Bill Cosby show, if the opening action takes place in the living room, then goes to the Cosbys' bedroom, then back to the living room, the cast goes back and forth in these sets with the cameras moving and the audience waiting while lighting is set up each time, and also waiting for any changes of cast costume. These waits can take over fifteen minutes each, and almost all series using this technique usually have a small orchestra and/or a "warm-up" comic to entertain between scenes and explain to the waiting viewers the reason for the delay and what is taking place. The warm-up man can be a young stand-up comic who specializes in this field. It also can be one of the performers, or producers of the show. Garry Marshall and Norman Lear would frequently act in this capacity. However, no matter how clever or important the warm-up person might be, if the episode takes too long to film, people start leaving. If a program runs exceptionally long because of numerous scene and costume changes, you can wind up with less than half the audience that was with you at the start.

The advantages of the one-camera method is that the show is "opened up." You can go on location if the script calls for it. We did several such shows during my eight year tenure with Lucille Ball. One where she visited Marineland and naturally wound up swimming with seals and having porpoises leap over her. We did a quartet of episodes showing Lucy trying to enroll her son Craig (Desi Arnaz, Jr.) in the Air Force Academy, culminating in a wild rubber raft ride down the Colorado River, something that could hardly be shot in front of an audience.

Another factor favoring the one-camera show is that the performers need not memorize an entire script, just the scene that is being filmed. In addition, these scenes need not be shot in one continuous take but can be broken down into short sequences, and if the performer blows a short scene, it can be done over again. In movies, some of these takes might be filmed dozens of times. In TV, because of low budgets and high blood pressure, three or four takes are the limit.

In the three-camera system, entire scenes, lasting several minutes, are frequently shot in one take. The main limitation is that the scenes don't run longer than the amount of film in the cameras, usually nine minutes. On the rare occasion when this does happen, we look for a suitable moment where the action can stop till the cameras are reloaded.

Sometimes the continuity is interrupted because a performer blows a speech badly or commits some other gaffe and the scene is reshot immediately. The studio audience is usually informed as to the reason for redoing it, in a humorous way if possible, and they are frequently admonished, "Remember where you laughed before and please laugh again in those same places." And the audience almost always does— sometimes even louder the second time around.

What is the most vital ingredient in planning a series? Experience. You don't have to have a long list of credits or a thick and impressive résumé. As Yogi Berra once said, "You can observe a lot just by watching." Watch, watch, watch!

Watch the current crop of top sitcoms and compare them with the hardy perennials of the past, which seem to have endless reruns. You may find that their attitudes and subject matter have changed through the years, but there is one thing they all have in common: strong characters. If a new series has believable, even though larger than life, characters, in whom the viewers can recognize somewhat distorted images of themselves, friends, or relatives, then there is a chance of its joining the tube's immortals.

If the characters are memorable, then the series is hardly forgettable. Archie Bunker may have been the most memorable character on the tube. However, if Archie had been presented as just a bigot, I doubt if he would have captured the public's adulation. His creators were clever enough to endow him with several redeeming and endearing qualities. Among them love for his daughter and his wife. Yes, he loved Edith despite his calling her Dingbat and yelling at her to "stifle." Remembering her birthday and giving her a card causing her to say ecstatically, "Oh, Archie, it's almost a Hallmark."

A show doesn't always have to have a dominant character or pair of them. There have been series with a star surrounded by an ensemble cast in much the manner a jeweler will encircle a large diamond with smaller ones, enhancing the whole.

Some of the best past examples are *Barney Miller, Taxi, Mary Tyler Moore,* and *The Phil Silvers Show.* There are dozens of them. Currently (the 1985–86 season), we have several successful shows that seem to fit into the ensemble category: *Cheers, The Facts of Life, Family Ties, Soap,* and *The Golden Girls* to name a quintet.

The best current example of a series whose star is *the Star* is *The Cosby Show*. The other members of the cast are all excellent, but the series wouldn't have attained such success without Bill Cosby. He was the necessary ingredient, just as Lucy was the performing force that carried all of her series to the top.

Do the networks know what they want? To some extent. One of their favorite phrases the last year or so is, "What do you have in mind for a breakout character?" A breakout character is someone who will immediately capture the viewing audience's love and loyalty, and one of the best examples is Henry Winkler as the Fonz on *Happy Days*. The Fonz caught on with the kids and zoomed the show into the Numero Uno ratings. But Henry Winkler was not in the cast when the show made its debut. Garry Marshall added him later, and he was supposed to play an occasionally recurring role, but viewer reaction changed that. Winkler's billing and income soared upward with the rating. He originally got fifth billing on the series and quickly went to the second spot. Then, in 1980, when Ron Howard (Richie Cunningham) left acting to start an even more successful career directing motion pictures, Winkler enjoyed top billing and salary to match. Another unplanned breakout character on *Happy Days* was teenaged Scott Baio, who made his appearance three years after the series started and turned his Chachi Arcola into the start of a successful career. And I guess lightning struck a third time for Garry Marshall when he introduced two blue collar working girls on *Happy Days* who soon were known to viewers as *LaVerne and Shirley*. However, the appearance of Penny Marshall and Cindy Williams as LaVerne and Shirley was a carefully planned strategy by Marshall to get the girls their own series via the *Happy Days* showcase. At the end of its first year, *L & S* was rated number two in the season's National Neilsens behind *Happy Days*. The following year the shows took the two top spots again, but *LaVerne and Shirley* was number one.

What does the neophyte, with no access to stars or producers, do when he wants to create a series? The same as the established names in the industry do. Write.

In getting a situation comedy on the air, the most immediate and important factor is the writing. If the networks, studios, or independent producers come across an intriguing idea that seems to have "hit" written on it, they are willing to advance development money. Development money is obviously money spent to develop an idea. The network or studio will pay a creator to devote time, fleshing out a brief submission that appeals to them. If they like the results, they proceed to a script, and then, if the Gods of Broadcasting smile, they make a pilot.

Pilots are expensive. They usually cost well over a million dollars to make, and only a scant handful of those completed ever become series. And some series, having been birthed by top creative people, featuring proved box office names, may only blossom for a few weeks. Some of these recent "morning glories" include *The Suzanne Pleshette Show, The Lucie Arnaz Show,* Ed Asner starring in *Off the Rack,* and others. Many Monday Morning Quarterbacks can tell you why these comedies didn't click, but they all looked like possible winners when they were announced. Like thoroughbred race horses, they all had good breeding. They came out of the best studios sired by top writers featuring well-known and beloved stars. And they didn't last a full season.

There is no disgrace to anyone involved in these projects. It happens to everyone. Norman Lear and Garry Marshall have had their share of failures.

The current darling of the airwaves is *The Bill Cosby Show.* However, this is the second series bearing that name. In 1969 there was a program with this title starring the very versatile and talented Cosby. In it he played a high school athletic coach. It received only mild reactions from viewers and lasted, I believe, two seasons. It's interesting to note that the first *Bill Cosby Show* was done via one camera. His current hit is performed with several cameras before a live audience. Also, he may not have had the right format, chemistry, cast, and writers the first time around. Whatever it was, we are indeed fortunate to get a second helping.

So how do you make a successful series?

I wish I knew.

The network and studio executives wish they knew too. During my four years at Paramount, I was asked to work on a pilot called *Hot WACS*. At the time, Goldie Hawn was a smash hit in the movie *Private Benjamin,* and every studio wanted to be the first with a comedy based on women in the army. I pointed out that Warner Brothers had TV rights to *Private Benjamin* and were shooting a series bearing that title and that probably wouldn't be as good as the movie because they didn't have Goldie Hawn. The studio executives said they knew about the other series, but they were going ahead anyway. So we made a carbon of a carbon copy, and Paramount blew a million dollars on what seemed an obviously doomed concept. The *Private Benjamin* TV version had a short stay on the air.

Still, it is possible for an outsider to sell an idea for a series. My suggestions are simple. Elementary. Start with a good idea. Something unique. A premise that hasn't been done before. A virgin premise is practically impossible to find. If your idea is somewhat similar in format to a successful series in the past, make sure you have a fresh twist on it.

Put your comedy concept on paper as concisely as possible, and then concentrate on your characters. Don't overwhelm the idea with a suggested large cast. Try to limit yourself to five or six unless you're aiming at an ensemble show like *Taxi, M*A*S*H, Barney Miller, Cheers,* or similar team efforts.

A short synopsis of what the pilot program would be should be included. Be brief, but make it something that will immediately interest the network or studio executive who reads it.

Remember, you have to introduce your characters, let people know what makes them click and tick, what their backgrounds are, and what they do for a living. Their occupation isn't always necessary. As previously observed, no one ever knew what Ozzie did for a living, but Dick Van Dyke was a comedy writer and his daily doings with his coworkers were a focal point of that series. Archie Bunker slaved, as he put it, on the loading dock, and moonlighted as a cab driver to earn money before he became owner of the bar. Lucy was a housewife on her first series but on her two subsequent shows, *Lucy* and *Here's Lucy,* she was Gale Gordon's secretary, whether he portrayed Theodore J. Mooney, bank executive, or Harrison Otis Carter, owner of the Unique Employment Agency.

These synopses need not be long. As an example, let us look at an imaginary presentation for the format and characters of the biggest hit of the 1985–86 season, *Golden Girls.* The premise can be summed up in a single sentence. Three ladies past their youth, but by no means past their prime, share a home in Florida and are joined by the elderly mother of one of them. The characters: Dorothy (Bea Arthur), a somewhat embittered divorcée who occasionally makes caustic cracks about her husband who left her after nearly forty years for an airline stewardess. Blanche (Rue McClanahan), a Southern accented sexpot, who, despite being a middle-aged widow, acts like Scarlett O'Hara trying to trap all the Rhett Butlers and every man she can. Another widow, Rose (Betty White), is naive and slightly more than scatterbrained. Add to this trio Sophia (Estelle Getty), Bea Arthur's octogenarian mother, who has recovered from a stroke and says the most outrageous and hilarious things heard on the tube.

I am sure that the creator of the show presented the network a far more complete and better outline for the series, but the skimpy sketchy roadmap I drew would certainly merit the attention of any executive with vision.

If you examine the characters, you will find that not one of them is 100 percent original. The sexpot, whether Southern or not, has been a comedic cliché. So has the sweet but dumb lady. Bea Arthur's divorcée Dorothy, sniping at her ex-husband, isn't exactly new, nor is the character of Sophia getting away with anything she says because of her age. True. But when they are all combined by an extremely skilled fashioner of funny shows, Susan Harris, creator of *Soap* and *Benson*, the four seemingly familiar ingredients blend into something fresh and wonderful. Perhaps in the hands of a less competent craftsman, or craftswoman, we might have wound up with a collection of clichés. However, Miss Harris gave a youth-oriented audience a series centered on older people, and according to the ratings, they love it.

Maybe you will be lucky enough to create a huge hit. Luck probably plays a part in everything. It's been said of people like Susan Harris, Norman Lear, Garry Marshall, and others who have several sock series, "The harder they work, the luckier they get."

Personally, I intend to keep creating pilot ideas whenever I feel they are worth the work. And when I feel lucky, I intend to buy lottery tickets.

XI
THE VARIETY SHOW

Alas. This vaudeville-spawned type of entertainment is moribund at the moment. Some of the most memorable series in TV's history have been variety shows. Milton Berle's weekly series popularized the medium and caused one wit to say, "Milton Berle's programs have been responsible for the sale of millions of television sets. I know I sold mine, and others sold theirs." But Berle did help make the medium, and he deserved the title "Mr. Television." Soon Berle was joined by many programs, such as *The Colgate Comedy Hour,* with its alternating stable of stars, including Danny Thomas, Martin and Lewis, and other big names.

As filmed situation comedies increased in popularity, variety waned, but varieties were still found frequently on the tube. Singers like Perry Como, Dean Martin, Andy Williams, and Glen Campbell headed one-hour series. Carol Burnett, the Smothers Brothers, and Flip Wilson all hit it big. Rowan and Martin's *Laugh In* laughed the team into the number one spot.

Currently, there is no regularly scheduled prime-time weekly variety series. *Saturday Night Live* is the closest but it is aimed at a special sophisticated group rather than the all-embracing audience its predecessors sought. Bob Hope's several annual hour shows are strictly variety and always rank high in the ratings. Bob still follows the formula he and all other variety shows used since the birth of television.

Late-night shows, especially Johnny Carson's, still follow this format. Open with a monologue, do some banter with guest stars, feature a specialty performer, occasionally work with them, and sometimes do sketches. *Saturday Night Live*, despite its raunchier offerings, also follows this tried and true track.

When there is a resurgence of variety shows, and there will be, the biggest break will be for young writers. The producers usually people their staffs with some experienced veterans, but also take a chance on numerous new talents. Many of today's most successful scripters started in this type of creative environment.

Countless comedy writers received ego-building Emmy Awards for their efforts on variety shows. *Laugh-In*'s ten writers won them in 1968; another ten won them in 1969 for *The Smothers Brothers Comedy Hour*, and fourteen writers trooped on stage to receive the gold-plated statuettes in 1976 for comic contributions to *Saturday Night Live*.

Many comics are now doing occasional variety hours with material too blue for prime time, but all networks are eager to revive this art form and keep searching for suitable stars to head up series.

As mentioned in the preface, variety will come back. In the summer of 1986, NBC signed talented young comedian Jay Leno to a long-term contract, hoping to build a variety-type show around him. On August 16, 1986, the *LA Times* had a story about the Disney Channel starting a variety series. And when one of the networks comes up with a successful series, you can bet your buns the others will quickly play their perpetual game of Follow the Leader. It will be a boon to all writers.

XII
THE BIOGRAPHY OF A SCRIPT

There is an adage in the industry: "Radio shows were written, TV shows are rewritten."

Comedy writers are the medium's upper bracket laborers. This is justice, because they need the money to pay for their Valium, sleeping pills, and psychiatrists. In prime time you laugh at their hilarious offerings, but in the mornings and afternoons they are crying on the couches of their Beverly Hills shrinks. In the main they complain not about sibling rivalry or Oedipus complexes. What the patient doctor hears is the following phrases, with endless variations, during the dollar-a-minute, fifty-minute hours:

"First they took out the key scene of the entire story, then they switched a great character I created, a black policeman who graduated Harvard, to a homosexual subway guard, and finally they took out the funniest line in the script because the star's seven-year-old son said something they thought was funnier." The person detailing this tale of woe is a comedy writer, usually freelance.

Most series are almost always staff-written, but all comedy shows augment their supply by buying from freelance writers. And the freelance writers are the Willy Lomans of the business. They have to keep selling with a smile on their face, a shine on their shoes, a new ribbon in their typewriter, and an ache in their heart that goes with the territory. Because chances are that you will freelance before landing a staff job, let's observe a fictitious freelancer.

First, the freelancer meets with the story editor, script supervisor, producer, or executive producer of a series. If the writer is fortunate enough to come up with a fresh, intriguing story idea, he is given a full script assignment. Some weeks later he hopefully deposits his first draft and waits anxiously while the show's staff of producers, script supervisors, and writers carefully read his script, all making suggestions for changes, additions, and deletions. Since these suggestions come from experienced comedy creators, who are cognizant of the series' needs, the freelance writer takes their suggestions. He hates their guts, but he takes their cuts. He revises his episode to comply with their wishes, and some time later he turns in his script for which he is amply paid (over ten thousand dollars plus future fat residuals). Despite the generous remuneration, there is no genuine joy in his soul because he knows that the next time he sees his baby, he will barely recognize it as the child that gestated in his mind for many months. There may be a superficial resemblance if he is lucky, and the degree of recognizable material remaining from the initial draft is rarely a reflection on the writer's ability.

Again the entire creative staff goes over the script, giving it a final polish. Next, the producers review these notes, which sometimes inspires them to revise or excise entire scenes. They are all eager to improve it. Truly they are trying to make a masterpiece out of your effort.

Next, the producers confer with the set designer, who informs them that if they insist on using the scene in the supermarket, constructing the set will cost upward of $30,000. Can the scene be eliminated and substitute some descriptive dialogue between cast principals in one of the standard sets used regularly in the series? Can we have the actors discuss what took place at the supermarket without showing it? The producers excise the routine, thus saving a small fortune and costing the scripter a stroke when he remembers the blood, sweat, and tears he wasted writing the lost scene. (Where the hero, shopping for fruit for the first time, tested a honey dew melon by denting it with his finger. Only he put three fingers through it, wound up with it stuck to his hand like a bowling ball, and played this for physical laughs, and the topper was when the Italian manager said to him, "You make-a the dents, it's a cost you ninety cents.)

You mourn your loss, but the script is now ready for a reading by the cast. The cast actually reads two scripts. The one that is being done that week, and your wonderful effort, which will be filmed next week. They get to your script, which is printed on pink paper and called the Pink, to differentiate it from the current week's offering, on white paper, called the White, which was last week's Pink. Now more suggestions are made by the cast, directors, etc. A performer objects to a line because he feels it's not in character, or a comic device has been done too often, or a line is unsympathetic, or not funny, or the all inclusive "I just don't feel it." Several hyphenated story editors/script consultants/writers/producers are at these meetings, trying to save the script by ad-libbing lines to replace the offending ones. If, after several minutes, they are unsuccessful, they cross out the unwanted dialogue and mark a notation "JTC"—acronym for "joke to come." The writing staff, whatever their titles, will have a full week to make repairs, needed or imaginary.

Comes the final week, the moment of truth, the time of taping or filming. The script undergoes another cast reading, and once more a heavy dissection. Occasionally, autopsy would be the proper word. Faults that were not evident seven days earlier pop up like mistakes in a tax audit. Repairs that were made do not seem as funny as they were days earlier when first suggested. A hole in the story that had been plugged up in the first act results in a more gaping one in the second act. Suggestions come from the director, story editors, script consultants, writers, producers, performers, extras, script secretaries, cameramen, and delivery boys from restaurants bringing in lunch or dinner—or maybe breakfast. The original writer knows not what is happening and hasn't seen his script in several weeks, sometimes months, and he is still numb from the shock of the producers telling him they had to cut the supermarket scene. In most cases this is merciful, because many of his scant surviving original creative touches die here or at least go into intensive care. Few of those on the critical list will survive the full week of eight- to ten- or twelve-hour days of rehearsals. The original writer is now happily working on another script for another series.

The reasons for the many changes are numerous and not capricious. A line that sounded fine when read while sitting around a table may lose some of its vitality when the actor delivers it while performing the physical action that accompanies it. Example: An actor has to rise from a chair to answer the telephone—and the line he was supposed to say during this action is too short, so it will not completely cover his "cross," or too long so that he'll have to continue talking after reaching the ringing telephone. Either way, an awkward line for the performer. A substitute is quickly found, usually by the performers or director—but frequently not by those staff members hired mainly for their writing ability. They are busily repairing next week's script—and trying to get large laugh lines in those spots marked JTC.

Unfortunately, the majority of performers cannot be counted on to make contributions to the writing. There are exceptions, and an outstanding one was *All in the Family*. Not only did each member of the cast, Carroll O'Connor, Jean Stapleton, Rob Reiner, and Sally Struthers know their characters better than any of the creative people on the staff, but they all had an instinctive empathy for the show and an excellent sense of humor. And so did our director, Paul Bogart. Their corrections and additions may not always have been for the best, but they had league-leading batting averages.

On *All in the Family* we taped the show twice on Friday nights before live audiences, once at 5:30, then again at 8:00. Between tapings, the entire crew had a quick dinner and a rewrite session lasting an hour or so, in which we tried to improve any obvious faults in the early show so that it would play a bit better at the later taping. Usually this was just a superficial polish, but occasionally the changes were long and numerous, and I didn't envy the cast, which now had to expunge speeches and moves they had memorized and rehearsed for a full week and appear before an audience with new routines they hardly had a chance to read, let alone rehearse.

Producers usually extend the courtesy of inviting the original writer to attend the taping and sit in the audience. Some accept, but many refuse, knowing that there is very little left of their original offering. One writer told me, "I better not come. The audience may wonder why they're all laughing and I, a grown man, am crying."

So the show is taped. It is edited, dubbed, scored, and aired. Since the writer receives solo credit for the script, he accepts the kudos of friends and relatives who know nothing of his traumatic experiences. But he is still not happy. He knows he is due for the last and most serious stab in the heart. The reruns.

Reruns are a mixed blessing to writers. They are given a certain specified residual fee whenever the show is repeated. The first repeat on the network during the summer brings big bucks and little or no anguish. The deep hurt comes when the show is "stripped" or syndicated. This happens usually after a series has been on several years, and there are sufficient episodes to show them every weekday, usually in the morning or afternoon, either on the networks or independent stations.

A half-hour comedy show must be exactly twenty-four minutes and thirty seconds long. This gives enough time for the opening and closing credits, and three minutes of commercials. However, when a show is stripped or syndicated, an additional three minutes are chopped out of it to make room for more commercials. Evidently, fans during the day have more tolerance for sales pitches than prime-time viewers.

The slicing of these additional three minutes is rarely done by any of the creative people connected with the series, and the results are puzzling, to say the least. For syndication it seems that they indiscriminately excise the key plot scenes, which usually took the author longer to construct than anything else and was the cohesive element that bound the laughs together in a solid story. And should he view this truncated version on the air, the author usually wants to commit suicide retroactively.

It happens to the biggest. When *All in the Family* went into syndication, Norman Lear waged war against this artistic mutilation. Powerful as Norman was, and is, he lost. I know that every time I view a syndicated rerun of a show I wrote, I die a little. And when *Here's Lucy* was shown in its syndicated version, I died dozens of deaths.

One example will suffice. The first show I ever wrote for Lucy (written with Bob O'Brien) had Jack Benny play a man whose life was ruined because he looked exactly like Jack Benny, and because this made people laugh, he became a plumber instead of a concert violinist. The episode opened with Lucy appearing on a talent program with a supposedly trained dog, which not only didn't do any tricks but ruined the show. Next, Lucy needed a plumber. The man she got was Harry Tuttle, the Jack Benny lookalike. Lucy volunteers to get him on the talent program and proceeds to do so, disguising herself as an Italian gal with a sexy black wig so the MC won't recognize her. When she talks to the MC on the show, introducing her musical plumber, the MC keeps staring at her, saying she looks familiar, and she jokes about it. When the plumber, wearing a maestro's hairdo, so he won't look too much like Jack Benny, plays the violin, his bow gets caught in Lucy's wig and removes it, revealing her red hair and confirming the MC's suspicions as he tries to get her and her violinist find offstage.

A simple plot, but lots of fun with Jack as the plumber doing jokes about Benny's age, cheapness, and "the only thing funny about Benny is that he walks like my sister."

But, oh, the syndicated reruns. They cut the entire establishing scene with Lucy and her trained dog ruining the talent program. Then, when she appeared posing as an Italian sexpot, there was no reason for it. And the viewers must have been puzzled when the MC kept saying she looked familiar. And when her wig came off and he said, "I knew it was you," the audience watching the rerun hadn't the faintest idea of what he was talking about, and neither did I.

On reruns the original writers frequently don't remember routines that were laugh-laden in prime time and completely cut for the shorter version. And one veteran complained to me, "I wrote the damned show, and I couldn't figure out what the hell the plot was about when it was syndicated." I know that feeling. I guess Shakespeare had a premonition of reruns when he wrote, "The evil that men do lives after them." Only, it's not always their fault.

XIII
THE BUSINESS OF
BECOMING A WRITER

Breaking In

The paths successful comedy writers have taken to break into the business are so various as to defy meaningful analysis.

Budding humorists, some still in high school, started by sending jokes to newspaper columnists just to see their name in print. Norman Lear, Woody Allen, Jackie Elinson (one of the top writer/producers), and I, among many others, started this way.

Getting my name into Walter Winchell's column almost daily led to a job with a press agent in November 1933—salary: ten dollars a week. Soon I opened my own office, and in 1938, when Bob Hope was starting a new radio show, I tried to land Hope as a publicity client and wrote a humorous letter to be sent under his name to the nation's radio editors. I wrote it with a youngster I hired named Mel Shavelson, currently a third-time president of the Writers' Guild. Then working for $17 per week.

We didn't get Hope's public relations business but our comedy letter persuaded Bob to hire us as writers at a salary of $100.00 per week, *each.* Hope's staff during the ensuing years included writers who had tried seemingly every occupation.

Several had come via the publicity field. Al Schwartz was a lawyer, and brother Sherwood quit medical school to join the group. Norman Panama and Mel Frank came fresh from college. Jack Douglas had been a drummer, nightclub comic, and professional fighter; Mort Lachman started by sending short stories to pulp magazines.

Larry Gelbart supposedly broke in because his father was a barber at Beverly Hills' most exclusive tonsorial parlor. Gelbart Senior was a raconteur, who would regale his comedian customers with humorous anecdotes as he snipped their hair. He also extolled his teenaged son's ability. This eventually led to Larry starting one of Hollywood's most brilliant comedy careers.

During my initial five-year stay with Hope, he hired close to 100 writers, and while a good percentage went on to become super successful, quite a few soon decided to try their luck in other fields. At times, Bob's scripting staff was so numerous we made it a subject for fun on the program.

At that time we had teenaged Judy Garland as a cast member, and Mel Shavelson wrote a much quoted line. It was during the football season, the week after the USC/Notre Dame game. On the program Bob bragged that he took his writers to the game. Judy said, "I know, I saw you come in with a big mob."

Bob demurred, "Come on, I don't have that many."

And Judy replied, "Bob, when you walked into the stadium with your writers, you looked like Notre Dame coming out for the second half."

Bob Schiller (Schiller and Weiskopf) started in the army by writing humorous articles for *Stars and Stripes.* He used these to interest an agent who got him a one-week tryout at $50.00 on the old *Duffy's Tavern* radio show. Schiller's partner, Bob Weiskopf, introduced the successful team of Norman Panama and Mel Frank to each other in college. After they left Bob

Hope, they recommended Weiskopf to Hope, and Weiskopf joined his scripting staff.

Several writers started in show business as actors. Carl Reiner now divides his time between the two fields and also directs and produces. David Ketchum was a semiregular on *Get Smart*. Bernie West (Nicholl, Ross and West, creators of *Three's Company* and *The Jeffersons*) put on greasepaint before tickling his typewriter.

Garry Marshall made his debut as a lowly copy boy on the *New York Daily News*. He contributed anecdotes to that paper's columnist, Bob Sylvester, and augmented his income by selling one-line jokes to Jan Murray, Buddy Hackett, Alan King, Phil Foster, and others. Then he became a contributing member of Jack Paar's scripting staff, which led to his joining Joey Bishop's sitcom, and the rest of Garry's fame and fortune you can probably find in the *Wall Street Journal*.

When Garry found himself in the enviable position of having a trio of his programs the three top-rated TV shows in the country *(Happy Days, LaVerne and Shirley,* and *Mork and Mindy),* he began staffing his shows with at least a dozen writers of all colors, creeds, and ages, and both sexes. Usually there'd be at least one seasoned veteran, three or four scripters who had several years of experience and excellent track records, and half a dozen neophytes.

The newcomers sat in on all staff rewrites, rehearsals, and meetings. They learned while they earned. And many have become exceedingly big earners. These include Bruce Johnson, Brian Levant, Fred Fox, Jr., Winifred Hervey, and Lowell Ganz, among others.

Supposedly, Lowell Ganz was hacking a cab in New York when Jack Klugman became his passenger. Jack told Lowell his destination, and Lowell told Jack he wanted to become a comedy writer. Klugman suggested that, if he ever got to Hollywood, to contact Garry Marshall. Lowell did. Working for and with Marshall, he became a writer-producer. Then he went on to pictures. Among his credits are *Splash* and *Gung Ho*, both of which he wrote with Babaloo Mandell, also an alumnus of the Marshall Plan.

Garry took chances on anyone who displayed a good sense of humor. For instance, Paula Roth. As a child in the Bronx, Paula took dancing lessons at 25¢ each from Marjorie Ward Marshall, who was Garry's mother. Another girl taking lessons was Mrs. Marshall's youngest child, Penny, Garry's sister. When Penny shot to super-stardom as LaVerne in *LaVerne and Shirley*, she remembered her dancing classmate, Paula, who even as a preteener could make all her girlhood friends laugh. Penny suggested that Garry bring Paula to Hollywood for a tryout.

Garry sent for Paula, but because his budget was stretched too tight, he gave Paula one of the strangest hyphenate jobs in this strangest of all strange cities. She became a combination writer for *LaVerne and Shirley* and Penny Marshall's chauffeur. There was only one tiny drawback to this arrangement. Paula didn't know how to drive. So whenever Penny wanted to go shopping, Paula would sit next to her as Penny drove. And whenever Paula had to go to a staff meeting, Penny would drive her there. As Paula once said, "I may have started for low dough, but I had the highest paid chauffeur in Hollywood history." Paula rose through the writers' ranks on *LaVerne and Shirley*, went on to become one of the highest paid staff members on *Happy Days*, and is currently a writer-producer on *Perfect Strangers*.

So how does a new writer start? The best way is to get an agent. How do you get an agent? This is a "Which came first, the chicken or the egg?" proposition. To get an agent you must have credits. Credits involve selling scripts or working on the staff of a show—a position usually gotten for you by an agent. In the Writers' Guild monthly *Newsletter*, they list all the series and their script requirements. Some of these shows have notations that they will read submissions from nonstaff writers, but only if they are presented via recognized agents.

The big, powerful agencies rarely handle beginners. In 1963, when I was head writer and producer of the Joey Bishop sitcom, one such beginner caught my attention. I thought he was a bright young man with a future. And although his salary was only $400 a week, less than luxurious at the time, I persuaded my agent, Joel Cohen, to take an interest in this youngster's future. Joel is currently one of the executives of the Sy Fischer Agency, a subsidiary of the Taft Broadcasting Company, and one of the biggest clients they handle is this young man. Garry Marshall.

If you cannot get a big agent to handle you, then try the smaller agencies. Often they are willing to interview young ambitious writers in hopes that they may be fostering and getting a percentage on the careers of a future Garry Marshall, Norman Lear, Susan Harris, Ed Weinberger, or any other potential giant.

If you are unable to get an agent, do not fret too much. Many unrepresented writers have gotten their first break through ingenuity. They have used diverse routes to attract the attention of various producers. Here are some of the methods created by others to get interviews with producers.

One inventive amateur had his résumé printed as though it were a fine wine label. He then pasted this label on bottles of wine, which he sent in to producers as his calling card. Whether the producer was a souse or the offspring of an ardent member of the WCTU, they recognized the working of a creative mind, and he did get many interviews.

Another young man was in a correctional institution of a large state when he began sending letters to every person whose name he saw listed as a producer on a comedy show. His stationery had a neatly drawn caricature of a man smiling through the bars of a prison cell. Several recipients of his letters, myself included, corresponded with him and found out his crime was the all-too-prevalent one among teenagers: cruising in a car borrowed without the owner's knowledge or permission.

He had studied writing while doing his time, and his letters were written with the encouragement of the institution's warden. They also showed a marked aptitude for comedy, and upon his release he was hired as a junior writer by one of the top shows.

Recently, a very attractive lady sent in her résumé on the back of an eight-by-ten glossy of herself. The résumé was impressive, but even more impressive was her picture. It showed a very shapely body clad in a bikini. I don't know whether it got her any interviews, but I'm sure it got her a lot of dates.

If you are truly ambitious, try to get a job—any job—with a production company. No matter how menial the work, you will get to know the people in power, and one of them may take a fancy to you and read your material. Today, most shows hire gofers to run errands for the staff. If you can get this job, don't worry about the lowly title. During the early days of the Bob Hope radio show, the newest staff addition also served as gofer. So every night when we were putting the program together with Hope, he sent out our newcomer to get him a pint of ice cream with pineapple topping. The name of our gofer was Sherwood Schwartz, one of the more successful writer-producers in the industry. And on Sid Caesar's *Show of Shows* the gofer was a kid named Neil Simon.

If you can't get work at a studio or wangle an appointment with a producer, try sending him material. Chances are that he will not read it because there are so many groundless plagiarism lawsuits that the studio's legal staff forbids him to look at unsolicited material. However, if you write to the producer and ask for a release form, you have a good chance of having him/her forwarding one to you—and once signed, your material may be read.

A word of warning though, and this is my personal opinion shared by many but not all producers. Do not attempt to write a complete script and expect the producer to give it his full attention, or even read it. He doesn't have the time. And for your own good, you must realize that if the script you submit is based on a story line they don't like, your entire effort is wasted. Also, in writing a full script for a successful ongoing show, you are competing with seasoned writers and a backlog of scripts the series has already done. Inevitably you will commit mistakes that are avoided by the veterans because of their knowledge of the series' needs.

There is one final, and perhaps best, way of getting a start. This is the almost infallible method of knowing somebody who knows somebody. There are sons and daughters of writers who have become quite successful on their own. Kim Weiskopf is the son of Bob Weiskopf, and Fred Fox, Jr., the offspring of Freddy Fox, Sr.—and both of these young men have established themselves as writers and producers. Sherwood and Elroy Schwartz got into the industry because their oldest brother Al was a reputable writer. Sherwood's son Lloyd is a successful writer-producer of comedy shows, but Al's son Douglas defied family tradition and went into the dramatic field where he has cowritten and produced many two-hour *Movies of the Week* and has a one-hour series, *The Wizard,* which made its debut on CBS in September 1986.

But remember one thing. Friends or relatives may get you an interview or even a job. Then you have to prove yourself to keep it. This is best summed up in the old joke about the rabbi and the priest who went to the fights at Madison Square Garden. After the fighters in the first event were introduced, one of the pugilists knelt in his corner and made the sign of the cross over his heart.

The rabbi asked the priest: "Will that help much?"

And the priest replied, "Not a damned bit if he can't hit."

Money and Other Considerations

The financial rewards for writers keep growing, and with the exploding popularity of cassettes, it will probably continue upward. There is no doubt that when deals can be made with all unions and the price is right, a big-selling item will be current series and comedy nostalgia. When the public can purchase cassettes containing several of the best episodes of *All in the Family, Dick Van Dyke, I Love Lucy,* and many other series, there will be extra revenue for the writers. Those turning out scripts for today's top programs will doubtless reap rewards from this new outlet.

Perhaps that is in the future, but many veterans have seen the future come in different ways. It was only a score of years or so ago when "scale" for writing a half-hour situation comedy was less than $3,000, plus residuals, which seemed fair at the time but is almost minuscule today.

The Writers' Guild has kept the minimum rising. As of the summer of 1986, it was nearly $11,000 for story and screenplay. This is paid whether a single writer or team or more do the job. Sometimes they will use a writer's story but have another scribe do the script. There is a set formula for payments for this.

There is also a set formula for residuals. If first rerun in prime network time, the residual is $5,348. Also, if it is run more than once in network prime time, the same amount is paid. When the show goes into syndication, the second run will bring 40 percent of the $5,348 figure—and all the following amounts are based on that figure. The third rerun is 30 percent; fourth, fifth, and sixth are each 25 percent; seventh, eighth, ninth, and tenth, 15 percent; eleventh, twelfth, 10 percent. After that, every time the program is shown in perpetuity, it brings 5 percent. If you die you can't take it with you, but your residuals become part of your estate.

Every writer joins the Guild when he or she can meet the requirements. The requirements keep changing. At the current time, a writer must have twelve credits. You are given twelve credits for selling a full-length motion picture screenplay. You get three credits for each half-hour TV script you sell. Four half-hour scripts give you twelve credits. It doesn't matter if you do these alone or with a collaborator, you'll each be given the full twelve credits. Then you have to pay a $1,500 fee to join, and dues are 1 percent of your annual earnings, and there is currently a move to increase this to 1.5 percent. To a beginner this may seem a lot of money, but it's worth it. The Guild protects a writer's rights, collects residuals, forwards them to you, and sees that you get fully paid. In Hollywood, having a powerful organization that looks after you like that is vital.

Another Guild service is protection of your script, story, or idea. Before submitting it to anyone, you can register it with the Guild for a small fee.

In addition, the Guild has an excellent health and welfare insurance plan and a pension plan. And these are subsidized via a percentage your employer pays on your writing fees. There are many other Guild benefits, and I suggest you write to them for further information. The address is Writers' Guild of America, 8955 Beverly Boulevard, Los Angeles, California, 90048.

Other Jobs for, and Ambitions of, Comedy Writers

Most newcomers to the comedy field have their eyes and hearts set on the major sources of fame and fortune of television. However, there are many other places they can work while waiting for the big bonanza or when they are between assignments.

Advertising agencies are going in for more and more humor in the printed media and especially their broadcast commercials. Some of the more memorable scenes and slogans were frequently funnier than the programs they interrupted, such as "Where's the Beef" and "I Can't Believe I Ate the Whole Thing." These were created by copy writers with comedy minds.

An obvious outlet is books. Many publishers get out paperbacks like *Gross Jokes* and *Truly Tasteless Jokes,* which sell exceedingly well. About fifteen years ago a comedy writer named Larry Wilde got an idea for a book called *The Official Polish/Italian Joke Book.* The front cover had a picture illustrating Polish jokes, the back cover was used to show Italian jokes. Larry had some material but not enough. He went to a local college campus, set up a little booth with a sign reading "I will pay a quarter for all Polish or Italian jokes." Within a week he had more than enough. His double-decker book became the biggest selling joke book in the history of publishing, nearly 2 million copies.

Greeting card companies are getting out a vast selection of comedy cards. There are other opportunities if you dig for them. Practically all politicians, including the President, love to inject humor in speeches. Many comedy writers have added spice to our top statesmen's speeches. Heads of large corporations love to inject laughs in long, technical dissertations. I used to add a few smiles to the speeches of Burton Baskin and Irvine Robbins when they owned Baskin-Robbins. Mr Robbins recently returned to his firm in an executive consultant capacity. In January 1987, he had to deliver a speech and brought it to me to inject a little humor. I put in one joke I had heard as a true happening. It went as follows. Actor Paul Newman is a great fan of Baskin-Robbins Ice Cream and one day entered one of their stores to purchase some of the frozen goodies. He got in line directly behind a lady who was just getting her order filled. The clerk handed her a double-dip chocolate ice cream cone and her change. She turned around to leave and found herself staring into the famed face of Paul Newman. She became understandably excited and said, "Why you . . . you're Paul Newman." He smiled acknowledgment and again the excited happy lady started to leave when she noticed her hand was empty. "My ice cream cone?" she asked, "Where's my ice cream cone?" Newman smiled at her and said, "You put it in your purse." It was not an original joke with me, but it fit so well it was the biggest laugh of the evening. Example: Mr. Robert Sarnoff was speaking to the executives of the Corning Glass Company and was discussing the cooperation between the two companies. His speech had the factual line, "Corning Glass and RCA worked together in perfecting the camera which took a picture of the earth from a height of 400 miles." I added, "It was a very clear picture except where somebody in Duluth moved."

Another example: Mr. Sarnoff's speech discussed the speed of transmission of a new RCA product. The speech said, "It happens in a micromillisecond. This is the shortest measurable amount of time."

I added, "Oh, there is one shorter. That's the amount of time it takes from when the traffic light turns from red to green, and the car behind you starts honking its horn."

Both of the jokes above are old, but they blended with the facts perfectly, and the businessmen and technicians appreciated these laughs in the long technical speeches.

The most obvious alternate field for TV writers is motion pictures, and, conversely, many screen playwrights have switched to the smaller screen. Some who have made fortunes in TV have felt there is either more prestige or money in movies.

Garry Marshall wrote and directed the *Flamingo Kid*. James Brooks of the *Mary Tyler Moore* series won three Oscars in 1984 for writing, directing, and producing *Terms of Endearment;* Larry Gelbart, who started out in TV, now has credits that include *Oh God,* and *Tootsie.* Even in television there are other alternatives. You can become a producer, a director, or even a hyphenate. A hyphenate is a person who has two or more jobs with a hyphen between the titles. Writer-producer is most common. I was writer-producer-script consultant on *All in the Family.* There are many combinations. Producer seems to be the title most coveted by writers, and they are attaining their goals with increasing rapidity.

Garry Marshall in a *TV Guide* interview said, "Writers today do one or two scripts and want to produce. Milt Josefsberg who was one of my mentors, put in twelve years of writing the Jack Benny show before he tried his skills as a producer." Of course, the ultimate goal of any writer is to create and own a successful series. The shining example at present is Norman Lear.

Lear, together with Bud Yorkin, started with *All in the Family* in January 1971. They formed a company called Tandem Productions, which then became Embassy. They did *The Jeffersons, Maude, Sanford and Son,* and many others. In June 1985, the company was worth between $350 and $450 million and was subsequently bought by Coca-Cola.

Questions and Answers

I have lectured and taught at numerous colleges, conducted special private writing classes, and sat in on countless seminars and panels on comedy. The last half of all of these sessions was devoted to questions and answers. The most frequent queries were on "How to break into the business," and tangential topics that I have covered in previous chapters. Here is a condensation of others that were asked at almost every meeting.

Where do writers get their story ideas from?

Anywhere and everywhere. Usually, current events and

news stories are excellent sources. Also, personal experiences. Once I started to shave, pressed the gadget on the top of the shaving cream can, and it spouted an endless stream of lather no matter what I did to stop it. This soon became the climactic comedy scene with Lucy in a supermarket, where she wreaked havoc and wound up testing a large can of whipped cream she wanted to taste and soon covered everything and everybody with the goo.

Here are some examples of current events becoming scripts: A news item told of a child pinned to the ground by a heavy produce-laden wagon that broke when a wheel collapsed. The child's mother, aided by a biological phenomenon causing a rush of adrenalin, was able to lift the several-ton wagon. This became a program where Lucy lifted a three-ton safe, which had slipped onto Gale Gordon's foot. Only Lucy experienced a bigger phenomenon. Her adrenal glands got stuck and kept pumping, so for the entire episode she was superwoman till the gift deserted her.

Another news item told of a girl who was drafted into the army because her first name was Sydney. We had Lucy get drafted because her name was Lucy Carmichael, and the draft called for a man named Lou C. Carmichael. Only Lucy wound up in the Marines, and we had a great physical show with her going through basic training with a bunch of guys till the mistake was rectified.

When I was producing *All in the Family,* the *Los Angeles Times* ran a series exposing private clubs, which barred minorities from membership. A script was written in which Archie Bunker's strictly restricted lodge was told to take in a Jew and a black or it would lose its meeting place in a public building. The solution was to admit just one member who happened to be a black Jew, and the results were excellent.

Do you watch comedy shows other than yours?

Yes, and you should watch them all. The good ones give you something to shoot at. The bad ones give you confidence. You can learn from everything. I discovered this as a school boy reading a biography of Thomas Alva Edison. When Edison was inventing the incandescent electric lightbulb, he tried numerous substances for the filament that would glow. He used silk, charcoal, various metals, and had over 150 failures before succeeding. He was asked, "Weren't you discouraged by all those failures?" Edison replied, "I had no failures. I learned 150 things that wouldn't work." For a writer it is imperative to know the things that won't work as well as those that will.

Do writers suffer from network interference?

Yes, but in indirect ratio to the ratings of their series. No one is going to tell *The Bill Cosby Show* people how to write, or what to do in their programs. However, the lower your rating the more advice you get. Occasionally it is valuable, but usually they point out faults you already recognize. A well-known incident took place during the days of radio, when Fred Allen just completed a mediocre—for him—broadcast. A network executive had been in the booth taking copious notes, and immediately after the program went off the air, began reading his criticisms of the script to Allen. Fred listened patiently for a few minutes and then quietly asked, "Where the hell were you when the pages were blank?"

I have read articles that situation comedy is dying. What do you think?

I've been reading items like that year after year throughout my career, and the answer is a definite "NO!" The stories reappear every time some different type program surges in popularity. The prime-time big money giveaway quiz programs were supposed to replace comedy. Then came all the Westerns: *Gunsmoke, Bonanza, Wagon Train,* etc. The shows concerning doctors and lawyers were supposed to replace the laugh getters. And most recently the prime-time soap operas.

On May 28, 1984, United Press International had a story in many papers that carried the doleful headline "Sitcoms' Decline No Laughing Matter." A month later, *Daily Variety* quoted CBS V.P. Harvey Shephard in a story saying, "TV Sitcoms Stuck in Rut." But at the same time NBC's Brandon Tartikoff was saying, "The network that is number one in comedy will be number one." Tartikoff was a helluva prophet, because he said this in the spring of 1984—months before *The Bill Cosby Show* hit the airwaves. Currently, winter of 1987, NBC is number one. *Cosby* and *Family Ties* are NBC's one-two punch in the Neilsens, and the great majority of the top twenty shows are comedies.

Has it ever happened that two writers submit almost identical plots for stories?

Frequently. On *All in the Family,* when Mike and Gloria moved to the house next door, the Bunkers were left with an empty room, and immediately we were flooded with dozens of ideas about who they would take in as a boarder.

What do writers do when they're out of work?

Write! Most of us try to come up with new ideas for series, screenplays, etc. The writer has one big advantage over the actor, director, and producer. Each of these three needs a vehicle to act in, direct, or produce. The writer creates his own work, and a period of unemployment should not shut down his creative juices.

I know I can write funny but my grammar, punctuation, and spelling are lousy. Will this be a hindrance?

Not likely. Viewers don't hear punctuation. That holds true too as far as spelling is concerned. Console yourself with Mark Twain's statement that in essence went, "I have no respect for a person who can't spell a word more than one way."

Many cities have places like the Comedy Store, or the Improv where young comedians try out. Are there any such places for writers?

To my knowledge, no. But as indicated at the start of this chapter, many colleges give courses in writing, and there are some privately run classes in comedy writing where you can go, meet others with similar interests, and pick up pointers on the craft. Another suggestion: If you know places like the Comedy Store, visit them as often as you can. You may see one or two talents that you think you can write for. Approach them. Suggest doing material for them. Some may be glad to have you. There will probably be little or no compensation at first, but think of it as homework. Also, some of our biggest stars started there. Think how fortunate it would be to hook up with a Robin Williams, who made his early start at the Comedy Store.

Do you watch dramatic shows as well as comedy?

Definitely. Only a thin line separates comedy and drama, and today's market seems to be going more and more for laugh shows with meaningful themes.

What makes certain shows hits and others flops?

Only God knows, and He rarely talks to writers. The networks make many comedy pilots each year, at astronomical costs, which never become series. They are usually shown one time only during the summer months. These pilots have been culled from hundreds of expensive scripts, which rarely become pilots. And then the mortality rate of new series is enormous.

The viewing public is the sole judge. Programs panned by critics have become hits. Conversely, there have been some programs praised by the press, which were dropped after one season. These included *He and She* with Paula Prentiss and Richard Benjamin, and more recently, *E.R.*, which starred Elliot Gould.

But even the public doesn't always know what it really wants. When *The Ropers* was spun off from *Three's Company* in March of 1979, it opened with possibly the highest Neilsen rating of any new show in history. And then, just as meteorically, it fell and was soon canceled.

Do you have to do much research in writing a script?

Definitely, especially when dealing with a medical subject. On *All in the Family* I wrote (with Ben Starr) the script where

Gloria has baby Joey. Several shows were predicated on the fact that Gloria was going to use natural childbirth or the LaMaze method, and we, plus everyone on staff, had to read several books on the subject and watch a short movie showing a young and attractive mother going through natural childbirth. We watched this movie quite squeamishly as the mother-to-be went through the pangs of labor. Finally, we were happy to see the head emerge and the doctor say in reassuring terms, "The head is out—ah, it's beautiful, beautiful." The still straining mother asked eagerly, "Is it a boy or a girl?" And the doctor answered, "I can't tell from just the ears." With permission, we used this line in the script, and it was one of the biggest laughs on the program.

Which is easier for a writer, comedy or drama?

I have no expertise on the latter. However, I can give you one famous quote usually attributed to famed character actor Edmund Gwenn. He was dying, and his friends were holding a deathwatch at his bed and discussing the impending end. One of them asked, "Tell me, Edmund, is dying hard?"

Gwenn thought for a moment and said, "Yes . . . but not as hard as doing comedy."

XIV
EXERCISES

Skeleton Plots

The best way to learn how to write is to write. Neil Simon has based almost all his plays on personal recollections, both happy and sad. His first success, *Come Blow Your Horn,* was a thinly veiled version of how he and his brother Danny (a well-known TV comedy writer and director) decided to have careers and lives of their own instead of their father's choosing. *The Odd Couple, Chapter Two, Brighton Beach Memoirs, Biloxi Blues,* and *Broadway Bound* are autobiographical.

Writers have turned out hundreds of excellent episodes based on things that irritated them because they knew they'd have audience empathy: Red tape. Computer mistakes in billing. Income tax. The interminably long line for a driver's license or unemployment insurance. The dreaded visit from the painters, plumber, electricians, etc. And one of the best is bureaucracy. The late Nat Hiken created a comedy classic some three decades ago when he was masterminding the *Phil Silvers Show* and had a chimp inducted into the army.

At most college comedy classes where I lectured, the students were told that while personal experience and universal gripes can provide the best premises or subplots, you soon run out of these, or they are not viable for the series, and ingenuity must be used.

Students would be assigned homework that consisted of each one writing a short script for the same show. The subject was created by the class and professor. I would rarely hear the scripts that were assigned during my temporary guest teaching assignment, but I did hear the ones selected at the previous session. The students would each play roles as they enacted these offerings. Because their scripts were based on classic long-running series, their parts were easy to portray. It was encouraging to note that, although all scripts started with the same basic assigned premise, their humor and approaches varied greatly.

For our exercises we will follow the identical basic formula. You will be given three skeletal springboards for scripts. Just enough of an idea to pique the interest of a producer, who is usually too busy to spend time on long convoluted story lines when the central gimmick is not sufficiently unique to warrant his further interest. If he thinks you have something worthwhile, you will have discussions with him and develop it further.

In the next chapter you will find these three ideas broadened, the story enlarged upon, jokes and other characters indicated, plus more plot twists. These would come about in conferences with the producer should your idea intrigue him.

These exercises, or homework, are based on three of the best-known series, which ran many years, and you are doubtlessly familiar with their characters and the type of stories they do. They are *All in the Family, Mary Tyler Moore,* and *LaVerne and Shirley.* Episodes of these shows are constantly being rerun, and you can observe the characters if you need to refresh your memories. Also, you can compare your efforts with their episodes. And if any of the suggested stories don't appeal to you, make up your own. And write short scripts for other series that may be more to your liking or compatible with your talents.

We'll start with *All in the Family* because it has four of the most sharply etched characters in broadcast history. Also, I spent five years on the series, one as a story editor, and four as head writer-producer-script consultant. During that time I wrote about three dozen scripts, and rewrote, with other staff members, over a hundred. So I speak from experience.

The thumbnail outline of the first exercise premise is this. Archie is very excited. A major brewer is running a contest in local bars to find the best pinball player in the city, with a new TV set being awarded to the winner. Archie is an expert and feels he can win. Edith and Gloria encourage Archie. Mike first scoffs at this dubious talent and then decides to help. In trying to help he accidentally injures Archie's hand, and Archie is positive it was done on purpose.

Exercise No. 2 is writing a *Mary Tyler Moore* show. We open in Dr. Smith's office. Mary is telling Dr. Smith that her mother insisted that Mary drop by and wish him well since he has moved his practice to Minneapolis. The doctor thanks Mary and says, "When I delivered you, you were a beautiful baby. And you still are."

As Mary exits, we see the door of a dentist's office across the hall. Exiting the dentist's office with a handkerchief covering his mouth is Ted Baxter. He sees Mary and is about to greet her when he spots the sign on the door of the office she's leaving, which bears the words, "Dr. Robert Smith, Obstetrician." Ted's facial expression tells us the whole plot. As Mary walks away from him he looks after her amazed and sympathetic, because Ted Baxter knows Mary is pregnant.

Exercise No. 3. A news story a few years ago told how Penny Marshall returned to her home to discover two teenagers dressed as Ninja assassins waiting to rob her. The report told how Penny managed to outwit the duo. That's it. A true happening that can be converted into a *LaVerne and Shirley* script.

So now you have three skimpy skeleton story outlines. Try to augment and develop them in your own way. Experiment with each character's reaction to the situation. Perhaps you can improve the plot. You might get a new twist.

In the following section you will find more fleshed-out versions of these stories, which I developed with no small assistance of several prominent writers. But try your own ingenuity before studying them. No peeking.

Fleshed-Out Versions

Archie comes home happy with good news. A local brewing company is sponsoring a citywide pinball machine-playing contest in bars with valuable prizes to the winners, and first prize is a huge TV set. As the acknowledged champ, Archie is going to represent Kelsey's Bar. Edith is happy of course. (Anytime Archie isn't angry, Edith is happy.) Edith compliments Archie and tells him he was always a good athlete and reminisces about his high school achievements, screwing up one or two of these memories.

Gloria and Mike enter. Gloria flatters her father, but Mike scoffs at this dubious talent, playing a pinball machine. He compares it with other useless accomplishments that men foolishly strive to become champions at. This leads to a typical Archie-Mike argument. (Archie, as usual, turns this into an anti-Polish tirade saying that they don't have pinball contests in Poland because no Dumb Polack can count over twenty, because that's all the fingers and toes they have. Mike might answer, "Oh yeah, the *men* can count to twenty-one." Archie would scream at Mike, "Shh, shh—don't talk like that in front of ladies, you pervert.")

Gloria takes Mike aside and points out that her father really has no other accomplishment to take pride in, and he should be encouraged. (Perhaps she quotes two famous sayings. One is that most men live lives of quiet desperation. The other is that each person in his or her life should have at least fifteen minutes of being a celebrity.)

Mike agrees with Gloria and now takes on the job of Archie's trainer. He points out that for every competition, participants, even chess players like Bobbie Fischer (whom Archie never heard of), go through rigorous physical training. They go through a regimen of roadwork and exercises as though training for a heavyweight championship fight. (Fun can be had with Mike making Archie do push-ups, jump rope, etc.)

They rent a pinball machine for Archie to practice on in the house. (The machine would have its back to the audience so that the performers playing it would be facing the camera. And special effects can simulate the noises and flashing lights of a high score.) Archie goes through his practice games with finesse and more body English than a belly dancer. When Edith tries her skill, she stands stock still thinking that she'd be unfair to, and taking advantage of, the machine if she manipulated it in any way. Archie can encourage her to use "body English," and a scene with Edith wiggling her body and becoming adept at the game should give some laughs.)

Edith might be upset because Archie is obsessed with winning—and Archie is willing to do anything to get first prize, a TV set. Edith tells him that his greed is against the Bible, "Remember—the Ten Commandments say, 'Thou shalt not covet thy neighbor's ass'." Archie can reply, "Edith, I don't want my neighbor's ass, all I want is a TV set." This can lead to a good routine between them, and scenes or jokes that further the story and are funny are a must in sitcoms.

(Example: We did an episode where Mike and Gloria discussed whom to leave baby Joey to if they should both get killed in an accident. Gloria suggests her parents. Mike adores Edith but doesn't want Archie to influence his son. Gloria points out that her father loves Joey, and Mike agrees but says Archie is absolutely insensitive. Enter Archie with baby Joey.

They had gone to the park. Archie tells them they had fun, and a beautiful little yellow butterfly with blue dots was flying around the boy, and Joey was so cute as he kept reaching to touch it. Gloria asked, "Did he touch it?" And Archie answered, "No, he was too slow, so I killed it and put it in his pocket." This was in a routine that progressed the plot by showing that Gloria was right; Archie would do anything for his grandson. It also showed that Mike was right when he said Archie had absolutely no sensitivity.)

Continuing our script premise: It is the night before the tournament. Our four cast members are at the Bunkers' house in a confident mood. Mike, always eager to eat, goes to the refrigerator, and Archie follows to get a beer. Mike inadvertently slams the door on Archie's hand. The hand of the champ. Archie screams the Meathead did it deliberately. Edith and Gloria sympathize with Archie and try to convince him that it wasn't intentional. Mike practically grovels, apologizing for the accident. The scene ends with them going to the emergency hospital with an always funny scene of Archie venting his spleen against nurses, doctors, hospitals, expenses, etc.

Now we come to the "button," the "blackout," the end.

Here are several different ways the program can conclude. Archie is at the bar, his hand encased in a cast, ready to forfeit the match, when in comes his opponent with both hands in casts as a result of an accident. Or Edith, Mike, or Gloria gets the right to act as Archie's substitute, and because of Archie's coaching either wins or loses. Or Archie refuses to concede to his opponent, an obnoxious type, who claims that Archie is faking an injury to avoid being humiliated in a game. The man then says he's going to run up a high score to show Bunker what he can do. On his second or third shot he begins "showboating" and tilts the machine, making Archie an automatic winner. Or Archie forfeits, but, according to the rules, his opponent must play a complete game to win. While he is doing this, the police raid the place. According to law, playing pinball machines for prizes is illegal in that part of town. They arrest the opponent, and when they ask Archie if he was playing, he lifts up his hand with the cast and innocently asks, "How could I?"

Those are some sample endings. There are probably many more. Try to work out a better one on your own.

Exercise No. 2 is the fleshed-out *Mary Tyler Moore* idea. We open in Dr. Smith's office. The doctor is a handsome gray-haired man, and he's thanking Mary for dropping in on him to wish him well. Mary said her mother has been urging her to do this for some time, and today she had to be in the building to see Dr. Kurtzman and take some allergy tests. Fun can be had with the type of allergy Mary has.

She exits and is standing at the door saying good-bye.

At this point we see Ted Baxter coming out of the dentist's office, with a handkerchief covering his mouth. As Mary exits she says good-bye to Dr. Smith and he says, "Good-bye, Mary, and I hope your tests come out okay." Ted overhears this, and then when Dr. Smith closes his door, Ted reads the sign on his door saying, "Dr. Robert Smith, Obstetrician." Ted looks after Mary, and again reads the sign. He has seen Mary come out of an obstetrician's office. He has heard the doctor talk to her about tests. He looks at the sign again and shakes his head sympathetically.

Here we have a ready-made, if completely contrived, situation. Ted Baxter, the world's biggest blabbermouth, has seen Mary coming out of an obstetrician's office and puts two and two together and comes up with nine months of pregnancy for poor unmarried Mary.

(Note: It is always a good rule for the writer to let the audience know exactly what wrong answer the conclusion-jumper has arrived at in his mind. It should be planted quite strongly and obviously, yet in such a manner that the "victim," in this case Mary, hasn't the vaguest idea of what is suspected.)

In keeping with his character, we know that at work Ted will be solicitous about Mary. He will pull out chairs for her, open doors, and even when she lifts a piece of paper, he will try to do it for her. Mary of course will be puzzled by his peculiar actions, and when she asks for an explanation, he will pat her arm and say, "Don't worry, Mary, I understand." Or words to that effect and will hurry away from her almost in tears.

At this point we have a situation that literally begs for the surefire juxtaposition gimmick. You can smoothly integrate a scene where Ted is busy in the background and another character asks Mary why she was late this morning. Mary answers, "I had to see a doctor. Two in fact." The other character asks, "Two?" And Mary, busy with some papers, answers, "Well, the second doctor was for my mother." Ted has approached just in time to hear Mary say she saw a doctor for her mother. In shocked amazement his mouth soundlessly utters the words "Her mother too?," and a couple of slightly double entendre misunderstandings can be exchanged between the innocent Mary and shocked Ted.

This is still not a fully-developed story, but should be a good exercise in writing jokes for a particular situation and how the various other characters on the show react to Ted's peculiar behavior. Also, as a writer, you'd have to decide whether Ted confides his news in anyone else—or does he braggingly blurt out to boss Lou Grant, "I know something you don't know." Does he let it slip by saying, "I'll never tell—not even for a million dollars will I tell you that Mary is pregnant." (Corny but almost a guaranteed laugh.) Or does he refuse to tell Lou, saying, "It's a secret, and one thing about me, when I make up my mind to keep a secret, I won't tell even if I'm offered a million dollars." And Lou says, "If you don't tell me, I'm going to dock you for being late this morning." And Ted instantly answers, "Mary's pregnant."

Try and work out Mary's reaction when she finds out about

it. Does she indignantly tell Ted off? Does she instead go along with the gag and pretend that she is, indeed, pregnant? If she does this, does it backfire? Does Ted try to protect her and say, "Tell me the louse's name, and I'll kill him with my bare hands"? Does Mary look at him in front of the entire cast and sheepishly say, "Why, Ted—how could you forget so soon? You're the father-to-be."

You take it from here.

For exercise No. 3 all we had was the brief news item in the papers that told how Penny Marshall came home to find two teenagers dressed as Ninja assassins waiting to rob her. Let's flesh this out a bit into a viable premise for a *LaVerne and Shirley* show.

We open with the girls in their apartment getting ready for a masquerade party that night. Both are excited because Rhonda, their beautiful neighbor, has arranged blind dates for them. "And let's face it," the girls admit, "Rhonda's castoffs are usually better than the best we get."

Laughs can be gotten from the costumes the girls are wearing. Perhaps mythical or historical characters like Little Bo Peep, Joan of Arc, Martha Washington, Pocahontas, etc. Sample joke: Shirley says, "I wish I had stuck to my original idea of going as Lady Godiva." LaVerne critically eyes Shirley's lack of bosom and answers, "It's good you didn't. The way you're built more guys would be looking at the horse instead of you."

Two men dressed in Ninja costumes come climbing in through the balcony window. Shirley is impressed and thinks that's a dashing way for their blind dates to come pick them up. LaVerne looks them over appraisingly and says to Shirley, "You take Charlie Chan, I'll take Bruce Lee."

The Ninjas take out their swords and demand money, and when they slash a sword through a table, the girls realize they're in trouble.

Enter Lenny and Squiggy in outlandish costumes for the party (perhaps Tweedledum and Tweedledee), and they immediately assume the Ninjas are the girls' dates. The Ninjas swing their swords at them, the boys think it's a joke, and the girls frantically try to warn them of the danger.

Two policemen enter with guns drawn, and the girls think they are saved, but the cops turn out to be their blind dates, and their pistols are toys. Their beautiful neighbor Rhonda comes in and starts making a play for the Ninjas.

What you should try to write is a zany routine similar to the famed jammed stateroom scene in the Marx Brothers' picture. It will not only be fun, but also good homework in writing a different style of comedy.

XV
CONCLUDING NOTES

Proficient teachers, either in classes or via books, can teach you the rudimentary skills and successful strategies of writing comedy. However, the best way to learn how to write is to write, write, write.

*   *   *

When you finish a script or story premise, put it away for a week or so and try not to think of it. Then reread it. You'll be surprised how many ideas you'll have for improving your first draft. This edict holds true for successful scripters. Most are never completely satisfied with their initial efforts and rewrite them several times. I have occasionally seen a rerun of a show I wrote years ago, and while watching a scene, I will get an idea how it could have been done better or funnier.

*   *   *

Listen to criticism, but use your own judgment. If five friends read your script and give five varied opinions, you have to follow your gut instincts. However, if there is a unanimity of opinion on a certain weakness in your script, it would be best to remedy it. There is an old adage in the industry: "If three people tell you you're sick, lie down."

* * *

Don't be discouraged. Almost every writer has had the experience of a story idea being rejected by one show and then winding up as a successful episode on another series.

* * *

Above all, write, write, write.

* * *

Good luck.

For Further Reading

The Great Comedians Talk About Comedy by Larry Wilde (Citadel).

TV Writing by Richard A. Blum (Hastings House).

How to Write and Sell Humor by Gene Perret (Writers Digest Books).

The Screen Writer Looks at the Screen Writer by William Froug (Macmillan).

Funny Men Don't Laugh by Arnold M. Auerbach (Doubleday).

Writing for Film and Television by Steward Bronfield (Prentice-Hall).

Origins of Wit and Humor by Albert Rapp (E. P. Dutton).

Writing for Television by Max Wylie (Cowles Book Company).

How the Great Comedy Writers Create Laughter by Larry Wilde (Nelson Hall).

The Craft of Comedy Writing by Sol Saks (Writers Digest Books).

2100 Laughs for All Occasions by Robert Orben (Doubleday).

The TV Scriptwriter's Handbook by Alfred Brenner (Writers Digest Books).

About the Author

Milt Josefsberg has the best track record of any comedy writer in the history of broadcasting. He has written more years on more number one rated shows than any other writer.

His credits include seven years with Bob Hope (radio and television), twelve years with Jack Benny (radio and television), eight years with Lucille Ball as writer, head writer, and script consultant. He created the format for her third series, *Here's Lucy*, which ran for six years. This trio of comedy giants scored consistently at the very top of the ratings, frequently number one, during Josefsberg's tenure. In May 1975 he joined *All in the Family* as writer-story editor and during the 1975–76 season *Family* was the number one show in sixteen out of eighteen national Neilsen ratings. For the 1976–77 season, Josefsberg was given a new contract as producer, script supervisor, and head writer. He continued in these capacities for three additional years on *All in the Family* and served similarly for one more year when the show became *Archie Bunker's Place*.

In 1980 he went to Paramount TV, working on Garry Marshall's shows as either producer, writer, or executive consultant. For two years he worked both *La Verne and Shirley* and *Mork and Mindy*. Then one year he doubled between *La Verne and Shirley* and *Happy Days*. For the 1983–84 season he worked on *Happy Days*. He is currently Executive Script Consultant on *You Can't Take It With You,* starring Harry Morgan and Lois Nettleton.

During his career he has won the Emmy, Critics' Circle, Golden Globe, Humanitas, Population Zero, and many other awards. He has received several additional nominations for the Emmy, the Writers Guild Awards, and numerous other honors.

He has lectured on comedy at several colleges and schools specializing in teaching writing. He is also the author of the definitive book on Jack Benny, *The Jack Benny Show.* The book received unanimous critical acclaim, and *Publisher's Weekly*'s review started off by saying, "It would be hard to top Josefsberg's entertaining and affectionate memoir of the man who was his employer and friend for many years." The book went into four printings, and is used by many universities and colleges in conjunction with their courses on comedy.